'But it is certainly a sacrilege to tamper with natural history. I appeal to you, film authors and fellow-producers. Before you produce or write animal films, consult authentic and authoritative books that have been written by men who have spent many years acquiring first hand personal knowledge of the primeval forests, the deserts and the jungle.'

– Joseph Delmont, *Wild Animals on the Films* (1925).

Table of Contents

Acknowledgements

Many people have been very kind in helping me research this book. Some have lent me books or given me links to the internet, most have trawled their memories, and many have dug out bits of their own family history including photographs, press cuttings, books, and even copies of films. Some have even spent time in libraries overseas, coming up with obscure articles and information. I thank them all, and couldn't have even scratched the surface of the subject without them.

Matt Aeberhard, Alison Aitken, Gus Akerheilm, Tony Archer, Jen and the late Des Bartlett, Peter Bassett, William Beinart, Caroline Brett, Andres Bifani, Jeffrey Boswall, Derek Bouse, Richard Brock, Monty and Barbara Brown, Cindy Buxton, Bob and Heather Campbell, Brian and Sheila Carr Hartley, Roy and Judy Carr Hartley, Gus Christie, Pat Cottar, Jack Couffer, Sophie Darlington, Michel de la place Toulouse, Mark Deeble and Victoria Stone, Tony and Rose Dyer, Mohinder Dhillon, Mark Fletcher, Sara Ford, Laurie Gwyther, John Heminway, Pascal Imperator, Brian Jackman, Colin Jackson, Kibaara Kaugi, Ned Kelly, Derek Kilkenny-Blake, Rudi Kovanic, Wolfgang Knoepfler, Charles Lagus, Richard Leakey, Brian Leith, David Maingi, Rick and Sally Mann, Hugh Maynard, Katie McKeown, Steve Miller, Steve Mills, Bud Morgan, Patrick Morris, Dr Bitange Ndemo, Andrew Nightingale, Ivo Nightingale, Barry Paine, Mary Plage, Jenny Pont, Nigel Pope, Reinhard Radke, Alan Root, Monty Ruben, Bob Ryan, Warren Samuels, Ian Saunders, Keith Scholey, Daphne Sheldrick, Simon Trevor, Tanya Trevor-Saunders, Barbara Tyack, Evert van den Bos, Heather Wallington, Adrian Warren.

I would also like to thank Professor Kimani Njogu and his team, my publishers, without whom this book would never have seen the light of day. Mia Collis deserves gratitude for designing the cover. I am particularly grateful to my lovely editor, Stephanie Kitchen who turned my colloquial chat into some kind of grammatical order, and made suggestions and improvements way beyond the call of duty.

Foreword

Jean Hartley's study offers a unique and rather personal perspective on a group of people who have, over the past century, made wildlife and nature available to hundreds of millions of people across the world. It is the historical context that I find interesting and the subject of filmmaking is not one that most of us know much about or even think about.

As a young teenager, growing up in Kenya and being the son of Louis Leakey who was running Kenya's National Museum, I came to know many of the personalities whom the author writes about. From the 1950s when my parents built a small family home to the west of Nairobi, I became a frequent visitor to the Armand Denis menagerie and often made pocket money from Des Bartlett who needed 'foolish' volunteers to handle some of the animals he was filming. I say 'foolish' because more often than not, the animal would bite the 'handler' in an attempt to change its predicament. I have a list of 'bite experiences' that include chimps, monkeys, bush babies, mongoose, spiders and not very venomous snakes. It was great fun for sure and I made enough money to avoid asking my parents for cash that I needed to impress my limited circle of might be girlfriends.

I am of the view that Armand Denis was a critical factor in bringing African wildlife to the screen. But it was Des Bartlett who took the opportunity that Armand provided, to mentor and encourage early cameramen who went on and have themselves inspired others. Des, Alan, Simon, Hugo and Bob have all played key roles that few people know about and this book provides a glimpse of who they were and who they are.

Eco-tourism, environmental concern, conservation at the community level, support for the national parks of Africa, and an awakening of the global community to the challenges of climate change on a global scale are all areas where good wildlife documentaries have brought changes to people's attitudes. It is fair to say that a few little-recognized men and women, over a period of a century, have made an enormous difference. The filmmakers are the unsung heroes and I am delighted that within the pages that follow a beginning has been made to recognise them. Popular concern for wildlife and nature cannot be taken for granted. Inspired filming and presentation must continue and I would say that the bar has been set high.

I am personally grateful to Jean Hartley, a friend for many years, for taking the time to remind us.

Richard Leakey, FRS
May 2010

Introduction

'They are a race apart. Common sense is a commodity they have little use for. They are attracted by the grandiose and the irrational. Sometimes the consequences are ludicrous.' – Michaela Denis, Leopard in my Lap (1955).

Africa has been described as the most exciting continent on the planet. Elspeth Huxley, one of Kenya's most prolific writers, wrote 'Kenya must be the most photographed country in the world'. With a history of over a hundred years of such a variety of safari visitors arriving to experience and photograph the country's immense variety of attractions, it would be hard to contradict her.

This book is intended to tell the story of wildlife films in East Africa through the twentieth century. Photographers with cumbersome stills cameras arrived in the country late in the nineteenth century, but it has usually been accepted that the first moving film in Kenya was made in 1909 by Cherry Kearton, a Yorkshireman, who together with his brother Richard, pioneered the filming of birds in Britain. Cherry was asked to join Theodore Roosevelt briefly on his epic safari for the Smithsonian Museum in 1909, to record part of his expedition on film. This became *Roosevelt in Africa* and *TR in Africa* and was shown in New York and London cinemas after the event. However, there were certainly other people with movie cameras in Kenya in 1909, so I am not entirely convinced that Kearton was really the first.

The definition of wildlife films is open to interpretation. The twentieth century saw an interesting series of transformations. In the early years photographic safaris and organised mass-tourism did not exist, and most films of the time covered hunting safaris or 'expeditions'. These commenced shortly after the railway reached Nairobi at the turn of the century. The source of the Nile had long since been found, but there were still people in search of adventure on a lesser scale, who wanted to explore for themselves the mysteries of the 'dark continent'. Much remained unknown of Africa's interior. There were enticing places, people, animals and plants all waiting to be 'discovered'. To many people, 'wildlife' is a term that covers animals, birds, reptiles, amphibians and insects. However, 'nature' is but part of the entire complicated inter-connected system of life on this planet that embraces every arm of natural science – from evolution through palaeontology to climate change – so I will refer to 'nature films' as well as 'wildlife films'.

The activities of the few pioneer filmmakers, such as Cherry Kearton and the unlikely American couple Martin and Osa Johnson, were interrupted by two world wars, but many hundreds of films were made nonetheless. The Johnsons spent years at a time travelling and filming in Africa, but did not complete that many films. *Simba* in 1928 and *Congorilla* in 1932 are perhaps the best known. The Johnsons' films usually featured Osa (apparently) shooting a rhino, elephant or lion with a rifle after it had been induced to charge, while Martin rolled the camera. Their footage of people is cringingly patronising, but they were pioneers in their own way, and therefore part of this history. They were also responsible for bringing the world's attention to one of Kenya's most beautiful places – Mount Marsabit. The Johnsons set up camp on the shores of the lake they called 'Lake Paradise' and stayed there for four years.

Others have been written about before – Carl Akeley, Paul Rainey, Paul Hoefler for instance. But there were more – William Boyce and George Lawrence in their balloon, Pop Binks, and Charles Cottar all contributed in some way. As well as reading their own books, I have delved into the records of the old professional hunters and safari operators. After all, none of the early film makers would have got out of Nairobi without an 'outfitter'. These people may not have been particularly literate, but at least they knew where they were going, and they knew more about the wildlife and the people. In this way, the 'Kenya point of view' is revealed.

If the human race indeed originated in East Africa, so too did a special breed of filmmaker. In my mind, five outstanding filmmakers (three of them still very much alive and living in Kenya) who all started filming more than fifty years ago, set the standard for the nature films that are being made today. The fact that they lived here permanently meant that they had more time to devote to filming – many of their films were put together over a period of several years. Not only did they have more time to film, but they also had more time to study their subjects, and it is patently obvious that the best wildlife films are made by people who understand the creatures they are filming. An extremely thorough and intimate knowledge of nature is essential. Joseph Delmont, in a book called *Wild Animals on the Films* published in 1925, wrote 'A nature film must be true to nature. Let it be entertaining by all means, and further it is a great advantage if it is also instructive, which does not mean that it need be tedious'.

I intend to cover all the major films that have been made in Kenya, and to include many of the thousands of filmmakers who have worked here. In order to trace the way in which these films have grown and developed, it is necessary to understand the various stages the genre has been through to reach where we are today. In the process, we shall see what makes a great film.

Africa's animals appeared in all the early silent 'expedition' films, and were shown in (mostly American) movie theatres, being introduced by the filmmakers who recounted their experiences in much the same way as lecturers make PowerPoint presentations today. When sound came in the late 1920s, the films changed and became 'adventure' feature films. The animals were still there, but there were actors and a story, however dubious – for instance in *Trader Horn* in 1931. This film was credited as being the most influential film to date in bringing the 'real' Africa to the screens. This trend continued after the Second World War. Into the early 1950s there was a sudden burst of Hollywood films featuring animals, professional hunters, and beautiful women – such as *Mogambo, King Solomon's Mines, Where No Vultures Fly*, and *Hatari*. All the big stars of the time came to Kenya – Ava Gardner,

Elsa Martinelli, Clark Gable, Stewart Grainger, Humphrey Bogart, John Wayne, Frank Sinatra and many others.

The 1950s was a major turning point. Television had come into being, and such programmes as *Filming Wild Animals* followed by *On Safari* with Armand and Michaela Denis offered a totally new way of watching wildlife. The couple set the bar at a new level. Their programme was very soon followed by David Attenborough's *Zoo Quest*. Now we were seeing wildlife for what it was, with no intrepid adventurers or romantic heroes in sight. Since then the wildlife film has grown and matured, camera design has changed beyond recognition, and people with passion have continued to amaze us with images that truly show nature at its best. It may have been a long time coming, but it was an interesting journey.

It will soon become clear that I am passionate about nature films. Having worked in this field for more than twenty years, I have also amassed a huge archive. My collection consists of approximately 14,000 hours of nature films, and I have watched all of them. There are some truly great films, wonderful films, good films, mediocre films and, sadly, some films that should never have been made at all. It seems to me that there is a problem here, and that the blame lies with two groups of people, one being led by the other. Whether it is possible to turn things around remains to be seen.

Interspersed in the narrative is what I hope will be read as no more than a delicate thread of my own life, principally relating to this broad spectrum of nature, people, films and Kenya, the country where I was born and raised, and in which I have lived forty years of my adult life, the last twenty-two of which spent looking after filmmakers. I hope this will not appear intrusive.

My Early Years

My earliest memories are dominated by animals, not people. Early photos show me with a cow, a horse, a dog, a cat; always at my happiest if accompanied by fur or feathers. Even in extreme youth, it seemed 'I loved nature more', despite being fairly gregarious. I recall my early days as being mostly in the open air with an animal friend of one kind or another, with grass, trees and flowers, and the sound of birds. If bad weather forced me to be indoors, then I was either surrounded by animals (stuffed toys or real) or engrossed in a book. Little girls are supposed to play with dolls but for me it was a teddy bear, a lion, a zebra, a hippo, a giraffe, armfuls of them. There was just one doll, I remember, and I think she was my mother's most treasured possession, handed down. She had an exquisite porcelain bisque face, real hair and eyes that closed. Lovely as she was, 'Our Monica' never really touched the same chord as the collection of animals that vied for position in my bed each night. Perhaps she was an attempt to instill in me a maternal instinct. If so, she failed miserably. She should have ended up on the *Antiques Road Show*, but sadly my 1999 flood destroyed her.

Early August 1955. I am just twelve years old and both my arms are in plaster following a fall from a half wild Arab stallion on the Brackenhurst golf course. At this time of year, my parents enjoy what is called local leave, and so we travel by train to the coast. As usual, we stay at the Sinbad, one of only three hotels on the beach at Malindi, a little town some way north of Mombasa.

With the plaster casts, swimming in the sea was not an option, so I soon set out to explore the area. On the other side of the road, I saw what looked like a safari camp, complete with tents and bush-going vehicles. Intrigued, I wandered across to investigate. There I found a rather gruff, tall man with spectacles and a woman with a cloud of unruly blonde hair and a strange accent. They were, of course, Armand and Michaela Denis. Also in the camp was a younger man who I found out was from Australia. His name was Des Bartlett, and he was tinkering with a camera.

I soon found out that my new friends had several animals in the camp, so I thought I was in heaven. Two in particular stand out –meerkats, which of course I had never seen, as they are not endemic to Kenya. They were affectionate, appealing, and had boundless energy. They needed to be exercised, and very soon I was allowed to take them to the beach. So for a blissful two weeks, I led Donald and Hogan to the water's edge each day and we walked for miles, chasing crabs. We must have attracted a certain amount of attention, a child with both arms in plaster and two endearing creatures playing in the surf, but I took my duties seriously and always returned them to their camp at the appointed time.

How was I to know that life would go a full circle?

The Beginning of Viewfinders, 1988

I entered the business of wildlife filming by accident. Taking on the task of organising an international birdwatching marathon to raise funds for a children's hospital, little did I realise that wildlife films would soon rule my life. Producer Adrian Warren of the BBC's Natural History Unit heard about the event, and thought that it might make a nice half hour programme. So, in addition to seven teams of birdwatchers, I ended up with two film crews as well. The event was well publicised, and involved a lot of logistics, appeals for financial support, organisation, coordination and split second timing. Teams came from England, The Netherlands, America and Zimbabwe, and all had to be flown to Kenya at no cost to the individual participants. Each team consisted of three people, so with the two Kenyan teams there were twenty-one birdwatchers. Most bird races of this sort are run over a twenty-four hour period, but as people had come from as far away as New Mexico, it was decided to make this a forty-eight hour event. In order to see the maximum number of different bird species (Kenya lists an impressive 1,078), it is essential to cover as many habitats as possible. The country is nearly a thousand miles across, and fifteen hundred miles from north to south. Altitudes range from the sandy beaches on the Indian Ocean shore to the snow-capped peaks of Africa's second highest mountain, Mount Kenya at over 17,000 feet. In between are arid deserts, dry thorn-bush plains, savannah grasslands, swamps, forests, lakes, rivers, gardens, cliffs, sewage ponds, national parks and cities. All forms of available transport had to be brought into play — minibuses, 4-wheel drive landcruisers, speed boats, aeroplanes, and even rally cars. Because the event was competitive — the teams were vying for a new world record and a handsome trophy — exact routes and locations were closely guarded secrets. I was the only person who knew each team's plan, and tried to ensure that none of them would be in the same place at the same time. To have three teams arriving, for instance at Lake Baringo, simultaneously would have meant that the one available boat could not have been used by everyone. Time was, of course, critical. Some locations were included with the aim of spotting just one species; then it was a race at top speed to the next place. I kept tabs on this by simply using a large map on which I traced the various routes with coloured lines. The map resembled a multi-coloured spider's web. Each team was supplied with a radio, loaned by the organisers of the Safari Rally, and was instructed to call the control office in Nairobi's Norfolk hotel as often as possible. In the control room, the scores were kept up-to-date on a computer, showing both the number of species seen by each team and the amount of sponsorship money raised. Each team was sponsored for the number of species, so the more birds seen (or heard), the more money was raised for the hospital.

The film's producer, Adrian Warren decided to enlist the services of a local crew in addition to his BBC crew. He also tried to get as much as possible of the event 'in the can' before the actual event. So colourful bird close-ups were obtained in many differing locations during the week preceding the event, as were some scenes of the different teams who were out on recce. It simply would not have been possible to follow all seven teams during the event, given the different routes and the huge distances involved.

In the end, the half hour programme, entitled *The Great African Bird Safari Rally* was aired just five weeks after the event – a very short time for all the post-production. One of the participants was Bill Oddie, the British birdwatching comedian, and the BBC crew had followed him round the race. It was therefore Bill who linked the whole thing together with a commentary in the studio. The event involved the participation of literally hundreds of people in Kenya, from hotel keepers to pilots, drivers to secretaries, computer operators, tour guides and game wardens. A very large proportion of the costs involved in publicising and organising such an activity were met in kind, and the final amount of money raised for the children's hospital totaled Ksh 750,000.

The day after the programme was aired, Adrian telephoned to tell me how it went down with the television audience and also told me that he would be coming back to Kenya in a couple of weeks to start work on a three-part wildlife documentary film on the Great Rift Valley. He asked if he could call on me for advice and assistance if needed - of course I said yes. And that was the beginning of a new career – I was then forty-three.

The Great Rift took two years to film, with crews covering Kenya, Tanzania, Ethiopia, Rwanda, Burundi, Djibouti and Madagascar. During this time I was doing people's accounts on a freelance basis, so was able to juggle my time if called upon to help the BBC. I drove out into the Rift Valley to check on an eagle's nest and transported 88 gallons of Jet A1 fuel in my truck to the Tanzanian border to refuel a helicopter. I flew in a single engined Cessna over the flamingo nesting colony on Lake Natron in Tanzania to assess the number of breeding pairs and age of any chicks, towed a Parafan on a trailer from the airport, and housed this extraordinary flying machine in my driveway for several months. A regular stream of BBC people came and went, often staying in my tiny rented house, where we also filmed a chameleon eating a locust on a tree at the bottom of the garden.

In July 1988, the last crew passed through to Tanzania, and I realised that it had all been great fun – something that is hard to experience when battling with balance sheets, depreciation, debtors and creditors. I felt that there was a niche to be filled, and that I could set up a business dealing exclusively with wildlife filmmakers. I thought that they would find working in East Africa much easier if there was someone on the ground to work with them – someone who knew their way around, someone sympathetic to wildlife, who spoke the language and could deal with the bureaucratic process of getting all the paperwork in order, who could go out and check whether the birds (or wild dogs or elephants or lions or termites) were breeding (or hatching or fledging or migrating). I felt that I had the right experience: born and bred in Kenya, fairly fluent in Kiswahili, extremely interested in all natural history, particularly birds, and a proven organiser. So, I set up a company – Viewfinders Ltd – in partnership with a girlfriend of similar background, interests and ability.

In my two years of working on *The Great Rift* I had learned that a wildlife film festival was held in Bristol in the UK every two years. Here, I was told, several hundred wildlife filmmakers gathered under one roof for a week to watch new films and compete for the coveted 'Golden Panda' awards, to arrange future programmes, to plan their filming activities all over the world, and to meet everyone else in the business. I felt the Bristol film festival was the right place to launch the activities of the new company, so I registered as a delegate for the festival in October 1988. I took along a brochure outlining the services we offered, and determined to find our first film client. During the week, I met several of the people from the BBC whom I had come to know, and they in turn introduced me to others. Everyone seemed most interested and encouraging, but the company was so new, and had yet to prove itself. I began to wonder whether I would find any clients. Then I was approached by a tall barrister who introduced himself by saying that he had just been on the telephone to Nairobi. He had spoken to a pilot friend of mine, who had recommended me. The barrister was Philip Cayford, of Pathfinder Films, and the film was *Ivory Wars*. I then met Richard Matthews, formerly with the BBC who had started his own company called Zebra Films, and he wanted to discuss logistics for his film on the Ngorongoro Crater (eventually to be called *Crater of the Rain God*). We had our first two clients. Both kept us busy for a long time, with more glitches and nightmares than we needed to cut our teeth on, but both eventually won Emmy awards. On my return to Nairobi, another client made contact – National Geographic was trying to set up a filming project featuring Jane Goodall in Burundi and Tanzania. They had been referred to us by one of the BBC *Great Rift* team. Having assumed that we would make our name on home ground before branching further afield in the region, we found that only one of our first three clients wanted to work in Kenya. Nothing ever goes quite to plan...

So Viewfinders officially started working in January 1989. We were off the ground.

A Universal language

Since it was at the Wildscreen film festival where we had found our first clients, I decided that I would attend regularly, and make the festival our principal marketing arena. So, another October therefore found me again at London's Heathrow airport armed with brochures and, by now, a longer list of impressive clients. I decided that I would spend a day or two in London before travelling to Bristol, to get over both the jet lag and the culture shock. The noise and pace of London and the demeanour of the people there always take a little while to get used to, so I opted to stay with a Kenya-born friend so as to acclimatise gradually. The Cockney taxi driver who drove me from the airport was the friendly, talkative sort, the kind that have a way of getting information out of you even if you don't want to get into conversation after a long flight. Before he changed into second gear he knew I was from Kenya. Before he changed into third he knew that I was in the business of wildlife films. After that, I hardly had to say a word. For this particular taxi driver was passionately fond of wildlife films, they were the only thing he ever watched on television, and he thought they were all 'bloody marvellous'.

In the autumn of that year, a BBC series called *Velvet Claw* was being shown every week, and my taxi driver had not missed one episode. 'It's bloody marvellous', he said, 'all about all them different animals, going right back to them dinosaurs an' that. Bloody marvellous'. I started to speak, to try to tell him that I had actually been involved (in a very small way) in one part of the series that was filmed in Kenya. But I don't think he heard me, he certainly didn't draw breath, and all the way up the Finchley Road he was enthusiastically raving on. 'Bloody marvellous', he said again, 'bloody marvellous, *all them animals evolutin'....*

I knew I was back in Britain.

What exactly does a wildlife fixer do?

'How many people can you get into an aeroplane?'

Many people ask what a fixer does. When I started there was no one who could tell me the answer. I am apparently credited with being 'the first' to legitimise fixing as a profession, so had to make up the rules as I went along.

It was logical to me that a wildlife film producer should be concentrating on his or her film, and not wasting time getting bogged down with bureaucracy, permits, licences, and regulations. In the early days, crews usually included a production assistant who was supposed to deal with these things. Very often she had to make decisions – where to book the crew's accommodation, where to hire a vehicle, how to plan the filming itinerary. Most often these decisions were not the best. It struck me that this was a job for someone local, with friends and contacts, with knowledge of the country's geography, wildlife, and also an understanding of the language. I knew Kenya well, having lived here all my life, and I had friends all over the country. I had been in the 'safari' business for a while, and therefore knew the country intimately, and knew which were the most reliable car hire companies and air charter companies, and where were the best places to stay. I had also worked in government for some years, so was familiar with much of the red tape that the British had left behind when Kenya gained independence in 1963, which has been breeding ever since. It seemed to me that film producers would benefit from having me on the ground as part of the team, playing the role of production assistant, location manager, travel agent, collector of paperwork, personal shopper, and whatever else was needed, rather than having to bring someone with them who did not know the country or how things worked.

Every film crew is different, every film has its own individual requirements, every producer works in a different way. It was therefore quite a steep learning curve in the early years. Producers did not (and some still do not) know what to expect from a fixer, and this fixer did not know what to expect from the producers. We played it by ear. I assumed that gels came in tubes, and did not know what a matte box was. They did not know how long it would take to drive from Nairobi to Amboseli, or what the roads were like. I was not at all sure what a fluid head was, and they were distinctly hazy about whether they needed special permission to drive off road in a national park. Over time they learned to trust me, and if I did not know the answer, I would soon find out.

On the strictly wildlife side, most producers knew what they wanted to film, and where to film it, but this was not always the case. Once I was told that a crew was arriving in January to film Verreaux's Eagles on their nest. I told them that I did not think this was a good idea, since these eagles generally nest in July. They changed their schedule.

Since I started fixing, others have followed, and there are now many people operating as I do, all over the world. So far no code of ethics for fixers has been produced, and this is something that I am working on as I slide gently (and ever so slowly) into retirement. It is important that everyone knows the rules, it is important that everyone sticks to a high standard, and I instinctively set the bar high, right from the start. At the Jackson Hole festival one year, I sat on a panel along with Jeremy Hogarth from Natural History New Zealand and Masaru Ikeo from NHK in Japan. I have forgotten the official title of what we were discussing, but it was something like 'how should film crews behave when working in foreign countries?' The panel and the audience discussed this at some length, and it was quite extraordinary that there were some filmmakers who thought it was acceptable to go to a Third World country, behave abominably, patronise the local people, get out of sticky situations by paying bribes, do a bit of filming, and then depart without paying their bills. Such an attitude can only muddy the waters for film crews who follow. Local people suddenly see film crews in a bad light, and the next one will not be made so welcome. This is not acceptable. I have to live here; I have to call in people to help, to share their own particular specialist knowledge, to become involved. If one of my crews misbehaves in some way, my backup network breaks down and can take a long time to repair.

Over the years, and over a thousand productions later, I have probably worked with more wildlife filmmakers than most people. Many are legends in their own right, some are rising stars and some are beginning to fade. We have seen them all, and of course we all have our particular favourites.

Obviously, I could not have done this alone, and have been lucky to have had some exceptional women to help me. My first assistant was Juliet Owles, born in Kenya, who could think outside the box, and would never, ever, let anything fall through the cracks. One day she came into work with a broad smile on her face, and I knew that she had met a man. He was a good looking chap from Naivasha, and in due course Juliet moved away. Her replacement was Jackie Ogle, a Liverpool lass with an appropriately zany sense of humour. Jackie was another hard worker, and we had a lot of laughs as we coped with some extraordinary problems, but eventually she had to leave the country. I struggled for a while, and then heard that Juliet and her Adonis had split up and that she was back in town. I chased her down, and she agreed to come back. I jokingly said I would make her sign a contract saying that she could not go off into the sunset with any more hunky men from Naivasha. After about a year, we were becoming increasingly busy, and Juliet suggested that we take on another hand. We chose Delulu Upson, another Kenyan who had been working for Kuki Gallman for some years. Delulu was at heart a country girl rather than a city girl, and spent her weekends playing polo. She was also a stickler for detail, and the three of us worked well together.

In early December 1999, disaster struck and my house and office were very nearly washed away when a dam broke upstream. The

Our Ancient Past

East Africa has always been recognised by palaentologists as the birthplace of mankind, and we have often been involved in making films about pre-history. Kenya's National Museum is home to many remains unearthed by the famous Leakey family – Louis and his wife Mary, their son Richard and his wife Maeve, and more recently their daughter Louise.

Because of their antiquity and therefore their fragility, several of the original pieces are inaccessible to researchers or film crews. The casting department of the museum, however, offers various models that have been cast in fibre glass from the original. It is therefore possible to order a complete set of the Laetoli footprints, a selection of mandibles, teeth and bones, or a complete skull.

When working with Granada TV for a series called *Ape Man*, we purchased a cast of all six Laetoli footprints. Flat on the ground with the edges covered by sand, this resulted in an acceptable and totally convincing sequence of the first proof of man becoming bipedal.

On another film, we purchased 'KNM-ER 3733', or Homo Erectus. The original, found by Bernard Ngeno at Koobi Fora, was the first proof that upright man had lived on the shores of Lake Turkana 1,700,000 years ago. We also ordered 'NKM-ER 1470', or Homo Habilis who lived in the same area 2,000,000 years ago.

My assistant Jackie collected the models from the Museum, and then went to meet the film producer at her hotel. Both skulls were carried in plastic bags, and Jackie ordered a cup of coffee by the swimming pool while waiting for the producer to come from her room. The producer arrived, and the two of them started chatting, waiting for the coffee. Coffee was not forthcoming, so Jackie summoned a waiter and said 'excuse me, I ordered coffee – please would you find out what happened to it?' The waiter disappeared again in the direction of the kitchen, and the two girls resumed chatting. Fifteen minutes later, still no coffee. By this time, the skulls had been handed over but remained in their plastic bags.

Not a smell of coffee. Jackie became a little impatient, and summoned the waiter once more – 'did you find out what happened to the coffee? Do you think it will come soon?' Once more, he disappeared towards the kitchen. He re-emerged a minute or two later, still empty handed. No coffee. Jackie took the matter into her own hands in her own inimitable way. She removed ER 3733 from the plastic bag and set him on the table. Then she summoned the waiter again. 'What do we have to do to get coffee here? I've waited over half an hour. Look what happened to the last guy who ordered coffee – *he's* been waiting over a million years.'

The waiter went white, but the coffee came very quickly.

building was declared 'uninhabitable' by the insurers, and we had no option but to move out. Juliet and Delulu were my rocks at this time, pillars of strength – they packed up all my belongings from the house and the office, organised transport and storage, and tried to salvage whatever they could. For a few days I moved in with a friend, but it was clear that we could not run a business in someone else's house, so we moved again. My vet Barry Cockar took my three cats and two dogs into his kennels, and offered me my own kennel in his little guesthouse. And it really was little. For seven months I lived in this tiny building, and we salvaged one computer so that we could keep going. Juliet and Delulu came daily, and somehow clients continued to come and go as if nothing had happened. Those days are now a blur to me. I suppose I suffered from Post Traumatic Stress. Without the girls, things would definitely have gone under, but somehow they held it together. After long negotiations with insurers, architects, quantity surveyors, and a contractor, my house was restored. This took seven months, and it was not until June 2000 that we were able to move back. Juliet and Delulu helped to reinstate all my belongings – the office, the house, the animals, the pot plants, to put everything back in its place.

Shortly after moving back, Juliet went on a long weekend to Zanzibar. She came back with a large rock on her finger, and that telltale smile on her lovely face. She had met another man, and he too was from Naivasha. She laughingly reminded me that she never did sign that contract. Off she went into the sunset again, this time for good, leaving Delulu and I to soldier on. Eventually Delulu was offered a job on a farm, which meant that she could be close to her horses, so sadly she left too, having worked with me for seven years. Malou, Adrian, Sara, Louise, Chania, Abbie, Joanne, Rowena, Kim and Sophia came to help for short periods until I found someone permanent. Now my right arm is Mia Collis, anthropologist, filmmaker and photographer extraordinaire. Bright, funny and hard working, she has like the others become a close friend and together we move into 2010 and our thousandth production. As to the future, I hope that the company will continue long after I have retired. We like to think we are unique, we offer a valuable service, and we hope we have contributed something to the industry.

The qualities required to do this job are many and varied. A sense of humour, flexibility, and an open mind probably come top of the list, and, in Stephen Fry's words, 'a touch of eccentric insanity' is absolutely essential. Living in a country where things do not always work as we may expect is no excuse for not being able to perform to an international standard. Our unwritten motto has always been 'never take "no" for an answer'. Over the years our clients have come from over thirty countries, and some of them work in mysterious ways, but we always strive to pay attention to every detail and to try to ensure that things go as smoothly as possible. I have always insisted on a serious work ethic, and total transparency on financial matters. Some projects involve huge sums of money, and if we are responsible for many thousands of dollars a year of other people's money, we have to be able to account for every cent. My years as a freelance accountant were, after all, worth it. No two days are the same, and we have been faced with some extraordinary requests – which is what makes it all so much fun.

The Start of Wildlife Filming, 1909

'Nature, red in tooth and claw.' – Alfred Lord Tennyson

Cherry Kearton, Carl Akeley, Pop Binks, William Boyce, George Lawrence

Most people seem to be under the impression that the first wildlife footage in Kenya was filmed by Cherry Kearton for the Roosevelt expedition. However, it seems very likely that Carl Akeley was filming at around the same time. Carl Akeley was certainly familiar with stills cameras, having bought one in London in 1896. The first photographic studio had been established in Nairobi in 1905 by HK ('Pop') Binks, and Pop very soon hired himself out as a cinematographer on hunting safaris. Pop therefore could also have been the first. Akeley did not set out to make commercial films, but he needed footage of live animals to aid him in his taxidermy – for when eventually he shipped the skins that he collected back to the American Museum of Natural History in New York.

Theodore Roosevelt's famous safari began when he arrived in the port of Mombasa in April 1909. Cherry Kearton arrived separately a month later, and it was apparently not until August or September of that year when they met in Nyeri, to the west of Mount Kenya. Roosevelt had just come down the mountain, having 'collected' an elephant, and Kearton was asked to film the celebratory Kikuyu and Maasai dance, or *ngoma* that was staged by the then Acting Governor, Sir Frederick Jackson. In the resulting film, the dancers were erroneously identified as Zulus. The level of ignorance about Kenya's people at that time is embarrassing, and the presidential party's knowledge of wildlife was little better. Roosevelt's party then headed north to Samburu, then Meru, the Aberdares and back to Nairobi before travelling west. Roosevelt's account of the trip does not state for how long Kearton accompanied him – in fact he only very fleetingly mentions the fact that they met at all. Footage exists of the presidential party crossing a river (said to be the northern Uaso Nyiru) on horseback, trailed by a very, very long line of porters all carrying 60 pound loads on their heads. Kearton's own expedition, with or without Roosevelt, covered a lot of ground, and when in Nairobi he based himself at the Norfolk hotel.

From the Kearton footage that I have seen, he was definitely in Nairobi for the launching of William Boyce's balloonograph in September 1909. Chicago newspaperman Boyce's plan was to film wild African animals from the air. In order to achieve this, he hired the top aerial cinematographer of the time, George Lawrence. Lawrence had achieved fame by filming the San Francisco earthquake of 1906 from the air, using a camera suspended from several kites strung together. Boyce suggested a balloon as an alternative method of obtaining aerial photos, so they brought two balloons as well as Lawrence's kites. The expedition carried 28,000 pounds of photographic equipment and supplies, including kites, collapsible towers, and the balloons. The test launch of the balloon in Nairobi was not far from the Norfolk hotel, on a hill the other side of the river, an area now known as Ngara. The whole exercise was fraught with problems, as their method of making the hydrogen gas was time consuming, not to say dangerous. Boyce had brought large quantities of sulphuric acid, and piles of iron filings and metal scraps were thrown into the acid, then the gas was transferred from wooden tanks to the balloon through cloth tubes (Health and Safety eat your hearts out…). The balloon was tethered, so that it did not get carried away. Large crowds gathered and waited patiently for a whole day, only to be disappointed. A second attempt the next day was more successful.

Also present were Carl and Delia Akeley, who had arrived on the same ship as Boyce and his party. Delia climbed into the basket and was carried some 500 feet into the air, winning the dubious distinction of becoming the first female to ride in a balloon in Africa. The basket was small, just 3 feet across and 3 feet deep. Lawrence went up with his camera and 'was amazed', but his photos did not come out. Boyce then got into the basket himself, but his 250 pound frame was too heavy and despite jettisoning his heavy boots, the basket refused to rise. It was then decided that the balloon should be taken to Kijabe on the eastern wall of the Rift Valley, where the winds were better. To get all the equipment to the railway station by oxcart took 4 spans of 16 oxen each, and nearly 400 porters, half of whom had been given horns to blow. So it must have been a rowdy procession. Arriving at Kijabe, Lawrence again tried to ascend with his camera, the balloon being tethered to a donkey and held by several strong men. The story (probably apocryphal) goes that a dust devil blew in, the men let go of the ropes, and the donkey was carried into the air, never to be seen again. Lawrence did manage to get some pictures from the kites, but they were not considered good, and he had no long lenses. In Boyce's words 'his big camera with six foot bellows that would photograph 100–500 yards is so heavy and long and takes so many porters to carry that you scare all the game out of the country trying to get near, and all he has got is one zebra and its legs are cut off in the picture'.

Lawrence tried to get some still flash photos to make up for his cine-failures, but lost several cameras in the process. He did not have a good record with flash, having once blown his young son out of a window after mixing the powder incorrectly. In Kenya he tried using flash on a male lion with a bit of tethered bait. The flash exploded, whereupon the lion charged the camera and destroyed it. The end result was that the balloon expedition was a total failure, and the only usable picture was a posed shot of two baby ostriches that an ostrich farmer had brought into camp. Lawrence subsequently abandoned photography as a career, and went into designing aeroplanes. Boyce returned to America and started the Boy Scouts' movement there.

Kearton filmed on the Kapiti plains east of Nairobi, then explored the Ngong Hills on his way to the Rift Valley. At some stage, he also filmed hippo in the Tana River. His travels, several trips, also took him to Tanzania, Uganda and into the Congo. The footage that eventually made it to cinema screens in New York was not put together in exact chronological order, and it seems that very little of it was filmed when Roosevelt and Kearton were together.

Kearton used Pop Binks' studio and dark room for developing his film. He also took along a projector and some 'animal' films. The first cinema show was a near disaster as Kearton's projector (illuminated by an arc lamp) did not work. Pop rigged up a barrel of acid water with two copper plates, which worked for only twenty minutes before steam started coming out of the barrel. The screws corroded and the plates came into contact with each other, thus blowing all the lights in Nairobi. They tried again, and managed to get it working for the second part of the show, though only for a few minutes.

After the balloonograph trial at Ngara, the Akeley party moved off to the Athi plains and the Tana River, and Carl tried to film a charging rhino. This proved difficult with the camera he had, and he built a 'rhino blind', described as being like a pantomime horse, but this was not successful. This grotesque blind was left behind, and found (and borrowed) many years later by Martin Johnson, but he too had little success with it. Both Akeley and Kearton had a real problem filming wildlife, as their tripods were static, their lenses primitive, and the action was simply too fast to capture on film. The heavy cameras were made of wood, as were the tripods. To operate the camera, the cameraman had to wind a handle, and this was noisy. If he wanted to pan, he had to move the tripod with another handle, so it was rather like rubbing your stomach with one hand and patting your head with the other. Akeley also tried to film a hundred Nandi warriors on a lion hunt, as Roosevelt and Kearton had tried before him, and declared the camera 'not adequate'. He therefore resolved to design a faster camera. On getting back to the US in 1911, he started on the design in earnest. Being a perfectionist, many prototypes were built and discarded, but he finally perfected it to his satisfaction and patented the Akeley camera in 1916, winning the John Wetherill medal for his efforts. The Akeley camera weighed 40 pounds, including tripod, and the head could move in any direction – the first proper 'pan and tilt'. The camera had 200 foot magazines, which could be changed in daylight, and the shutter let in 30 per cent more light than previous cameras. This camera was an innovation that changed everything, being waterproof and almost indestructible. Akeley sold it to the Signal Corps for use during the First World War, and after that it was adopted by Pathe and Fox studios, and used constantly by filmmakers right through the 1930s, when companies such as Bell & Howell came up with an alternative.

In those days, footage apparently changed hands frequently and so it is sometimes hard to ascertain who shot what, as everyone seemed to take credit whenever possible. Akeley was busy working on the specimens for the American Museum of Natural History (AMNH) Africa Hall, and this took a very long time (six years to mount three elephants). In order to make ends meet, he sold some of his footage to Paul Rainey.

Paul Rainey (1877–1923), J.C. Hemment, Buffalo Jones

Paul Rainey was a wealthy playboy, who was known for a flamboyant and extravagant lifestyle, including playing polo, sailing, fox hunting, tennis, and hunting bears with dogs. He had a 30,000 acre estate in Tennessee, and a 23,000 acre duck reserve in Louisiana, a racing stable on Long Island, a hotel in Mississippi, and he also bought land near Naivasha in Kenya. He decided that he would use his dogs for hunting lions in Africa, and arrived in 1911 with his hounds and two cine cameras, driven by compressed air. One can of air delivered 30 feet of film, but if the air ran out the camera could be hand cranked. Rainey hired Pop Binks to help him with the cameras, though he also had his own cameraman, J.C. Hemment. Rainey's cameraman JC Hemment was an established photographer, having been commissioned by the US government and several newspapers to take stills of various shipwrecks in Cuba in 1898. He had served in the Spanish-American war, so had unique experience of Cuba. He was also an accomplished ice skater, breaking the 200 yard record on the North Shrewsbury River on 24 January 1895. It was his interest in birds, however, that brought him to Africa with Rainey. Hemment is on record as being the first person to film aerials of wildlife – he filmed a flock of wild ducks early in 1911, possibly on Rainey's Louisiana property. He accompanied Rainey on the Africa expedition in order to take more moving pictures of birds, but he also collected some 150 specimens, which on his return to America in 1914, he presented to the Brooklyn Institute of Arts and Sciences.

I have watched ninety minutes of film alleged to be Rainey's, presumably shot by Hemment and Binks, and there are parts that are recognisably Nairobi, Samburu, Mount Ololokwe, and Archer's Post. There are scenes showing packs of dogs chasing a lion, camels being loaded, and several captive animals including a baby rhino and some young eland in a pen with chickens and goats. One rather distressing (and shaky – no tripod?) sequence shows a striped hyena with a heavy-duty gin trap on its hind leg, dragging a small tree, being boxed and carried off to camp. There is also quite a lot of footage taken around a waterhole – this footage could have been part of a film that Rainey released separately called *The Waterhole*, which was allegedly filmed at Laisamis in 1911.

In this same year of 1911, a character called Charles Jesse Jones also arrived in Kenya. He was an American cowboy, better known as Buffalo Jones and wanted to try out his speciality of lassoing animals in Africa. He was also the warden of Yellowstone National Park, and had experimented with interbreeding North American buffalo (bison) with domestic cattle – the resulting progeny were known as 'cataloes'. He brought with him ten dogs.

Now we reach a point that shows how a combination of badly recorded history and the mists of time can distort the facts. After all, any interpretation of history depends upon who wrote it.

In 1979 the BBC's George Inger produced a film called *The Wildlife Moving Picture Show* as one of *The World About Us* series. This film was presented by the inimitable Jeffrey Boswall, and traced the progress of wildlife filming from the beginning, i.e. from Cherry Kearton. The film contains many clips of Kearton's footage, including the well known shots of Roosevelt on horseback crossing a river. Then there is a clip, which we are told is from 1911, on Kearton's second trip to Kenya. According to Jeffrey's commentary, Kearton was asked by Buffalo Jones to film him lassoing animals. There is a scene with a pack of dogs surrounding a lioness, which look very much to me like Rainey's dogs. In fact, re-watching the Rainey footage, we find the exact same scene, same lioness, same dogs, but it has been flipped, so that the Rainey lion looks left and the Kearton lion looks right. A second Kearton clip in the BBC film shows the same gin-trapped striped hyena dragging its tree trunk, as is on the Rainey footage mentioned above, but this shot is from a different angle and obviously with a tripod.

Now, Jeffrey has been a film history scholar for longer than anyone can remember, and far be it from me to question his vastly superior knowledge. But I have to ask: does this mean that Rainey, Buffalo Jones, and Kearton were all together at this time? As far as I know, this question has never been raised before. The reality is further complicated by Gregg Mitman who writes in his excellent book *Reel Nature* 'Roosevelt publicly endorsed Cherry Kearton's motion pictures of Buffalo Jones lassoing wild animals in Africa at a preview before the New York Press Club in September of 1910...'.

In 1910? How can that be, if Buffalo Jones was not in Kenya with his lasso until 1911? Also in 1911, one Carl Hagenbeck, founder of the Tierpark Hagenbeck (zoo) at Stellingen near Hamburg, was in Kenya on a collecting trip for zoos, organised by the Boma Trading Company. Kearton was also hired to film this, but I have no dates.

Another BBC film about Kearton, entitled *Nation on Film – Wildlife* came out in 2006. This includes footage of a lion hunt, which Kearton had failed to film on his first trip in 1909 due to inadequate lenses. The (apparently 1911) sequence is taken apart, frame by frame, by one of the BBC's most respected editors Martin Elsbury, who reveals that the lion in question must have been tethered. In the same film, cameraman Gavin Thurston analyses a Kearton close up of a male lion drinking, and concludes that the animal must have been a tame one. So much for Theodore Roosevelt's reassurances that all Kearton's footage was squeaky clean and that nothing was set up.

Charles Cottar (1874–1940)

Charles Cottar was born in Iowa in 1874, and first came to Kenya in 1909. He liked what he saw, and decided to become a professional hunter. He went back to the US to collect his family and a camera, and returned to Kenya in 1913. It has been said that 'he left Oklahoma for Oklahoma's good' (but perhaps we should not go into that). He spent three years learning the business of hunting, and turned professional in 1918. He founded Cottars' Safaris, assisted by his sons Bud, Mike and Pat. The company was later run by Mike's son Glen, and now Glen's son Calvin is at the helm. Charles became proficient with his camera, and started selling wildlife footage to C.L. Chester Productions in New York. Early in 1920, Charles Cottar had a stroke. He also had several close encounters with leopards, and for some time was partially paralysed. In a letter dated 16 March 1920, CL Chester wrote:

> *It was with the most profound regret that we opened and read the letter from your daughter dated Jan 15th, in which we were informed of your illness.... Of course, your illness will seriously interfere with your picture making, hence it will be necessary for us to plan on other pictures from other parts of the world for release during this month and April. However, I hope your health will permit you to make pictures and get them to us for release in May, June and thereafter...*
> *I trust you will be able to secure ten or eleven thousand feet of very excellent material for us, making shipment of same from time to time.*

At this time the Chester studios were planning to move to California, but were to maintain an office in New York. Charles continued sending them footage right through the 1930s, and he also wrote press and magazine articles for *Field and Stream* among others. In the 1920s and 1930s, he frequently travelled to the US for lecture tours, the last of these being in March/April 1939 when he showed his motion picture programme entitled *African Wild Life* at the Glendale City High School, the Fish and Game Protective Association in Merced, and the La Brea Lodge in Los Angeles to appreciative audiences. The Worshipful Mayor of La Brea Lodge, Wendell J. Harvey 'instructed the Secretary of the Lodge to compliment Mr. Cottar on his excellent program, and recommend the same to any Lodge or organisation desiring this high type of entertainment'.

The Globe Theatre showed what was billed as 'the first movie of wildlife ever shown in the United States'. There was a film from this studio in 1919 called *Cameraing through Africa*, which could possibly have been Cottar's, but since the new studio and all its contents were destroyed in a fire, this is difficult to corroborate. Some of Cottar's film was preserved by his niece Myrtle, but she left it on a bus many years later and it was never seen again.

Cottar's several altercations with leopards resulted in him losing an eye and breaking an arm. Several times he went down with tick fever, but he continued with his safaris even in declining health. He had been to Marsabit in 1914, some ten years before the Johnsons arrived there, and his son Bud Cottar accompanied Martin and Osa on the Eastman expedition to Tanzania in 1926. Bud wrote that he was Osa's 'back up gun' while she was 'protecting' Martin filming. Mike Cottar led Paul Hoefler on the Colorado Africa Expedition in 1928 that resulted in the film *Africa Speaks*. Mike also had a camera donated to him by the Johnsons.

Charles Cottar was a larger than life character who from his early days in Africa appeared to respect the wildlife. I have found no footage of his, but he was certainly very critical of other filmmakers. In a letter to Archie Ritchie, chief Game Warden, dated 9 January 1939, Cottar wrote in no uncertain terms on the subject of 'fakery', or 'setting up' shots:

I have just sat in on a preview of one of the most disgusting pictures ever seen or photographed – was made in East Africa – I failed to recognise the land – or community – in the real disgusting scene – the mauling and killing of a quarter grown eland by a cage-reared lioness. The mauling lasted for hours apparently – and titles represented it to be a normal combat of wild-field beasts.

I often wonder, if something could or should not be done to have less of such preposterous stuff filmed in our country. Of course, the ordinary picture-going crowd knows nothing of the fake and naturally thinks it an ordinary occurrence – but to one who knows his Africa, the outstanding ribs on the emaciated animals assures him that the scenes was staged (sic), that the accessories were the farmers who loaned or sold for a song the half starved animals – to be murdered in cold blood to make a picture to go out and misrepresent the land we live in?

I am taking this up with the sponsors of this picture, in this country and wonder what help you may be able or inclined to give me from there.

A small 'trade mark' on the film, too small to attract ordinary attention read 'Roosevelt Expedition'. The party, a man and woman rode about in a white car, followed by a lorry.

The Roosevelt expedition films a sensuous picture they called 'Black Rapture', too full of sex to go well even here. They got a few remarkably good seens (sic) of wild rhino, elephants and hippo, but staged a scene of cheetah reared in captivity – after a buck in an enclosure – also one of a leopard killing a tommy also in an enclosure.

Why man, killer that I am on game as such – it made my blood boil to see these disgusting scenes; and had I in the field encountered the swine staging those scenes, there certainly would have been trouble. Years ago a padre filmed a scene out Ngong way of smoking a pet lion out of his cage to be speared by Maasai – not this disgusting stuff of staging a young eland being litterly (sic) torn to bits by an unsophisticated cage reared lioness – is too much to comment long about, and I sincerely hope you can run to earth this infamy and see if nothing can be, in future, done to assure no more such stuff is produced in our country – EA?

Charles Cottar was killed by a rhino in 1940, when out filming with his brother Ted at Barakitabu.

Paul J. Hoefler

Paul J Hoefler, from Denver, Colorado became an Africa hand in 1924–5 when he ventured on the Denver Africa Expedition to the Kalahari with Mike Cottar. This resulted in a film called *The Bushmen*, released in 1927. They obviously got on well, and Hoefler came back to Mike to plan the first trans-Africa journey from east to west in 1928–9. This was called the Colorado Africa Expedition, and resulted in the film *Africa Speaks*, released in 1930.

Hoefler, to his credit, apparently did some homework before embarking on this expedition. He said in his book, also called *Africa Speaks*, '

> *As Africa had always intrigued me more than any other place, it was natural that I should strive to prepare for my heart's desire; so I studied Africa for many years; its animal and bird life, its people and history; believing that sometime an opportunity would come to visit this land of mystery'.*

Hoefler and his friend Harold Austin arrived in Mombasa on 7 September 1928, having travelled from Denver to New York, then to Southampton and Brussels (to get permits for the Congo), and through the Mediterranean and Suez down the east coast of Africa. In Genoa they met Baron Bror von Blixen (Karen Blixen, of *Out of Africa*, was his wife). Mike Cottar met them in Mombasa, and having sorted out their vehicles they crossed the Likoni ferry to the south coast, and then proceeded to the Taita Hills, through Taveta to Moshi in what is now Tanzania. For seven months they travelled through the Serengeti and Kenya, filming all the time and constantly being delayed by mechanical problems, unexpected floods, staff wanting to go home, and allegedly only killing animals 'for the pot'. They were anxious to obtain footage of warriors killing a lion, and for this they relied on the experiences of people who had gone before them. They went to Kapsabet, on the western side of Kenya's Rift Valley and gathered fifteen Kipsigis tribesmen and took them into Tanzania for the lion hunt. On returning them home some time later, there was a victory dance in Kapsabet for the conquering heroes. They then ventured to Baringo and Bogoria, camping between the two lakes at a place Hoefler called Legumukum – this is now called Lovuenguen, the dialect having changed slightly. At Bogoria they saw flamingoes,

'one mile long and one eighth of a mile wide…. It does not seem possible that there could be so many birds of one kind in the world'.

They filmed the flamingoes, including nests, and then a very large swarm of locusts which ate every leaf and blade of grass in sight, before returning to Tanzania where they filmed giraffe, wildebeest, Thomson's gazelle and topi.

On 13 April 1929, Hoefler managed to tear himself away from all this wildlife, and the expedition set off west on their journey which would ultimately end in Lagos, Nigeria. They went via Mount Elgon to Uganda, to Murchison Falls, across the top of Lake Albert, and through northern Uganda to Arua. They came across a group of northern white rhinos, which were very heavily protected, and managed to film them before crossing the Congo border at Arua. Roads faded away, and much of the next part of the journey was on ferries down the Kibali, Bomokandi, Nzora and Yebu rivers to the Ituri Forest, home of the Ifi or pygmy people. At Wanda they encountered the tame African elephants, trained by King Leopold, then proceeded to Lake Chad. At Kiyabe they sought the plate-lip women, and the 7 feet tall Wasara people. From there they drove to Fort Lamy, Maidugari and Dikoa to the city of Jos in Nigeria, thence to Kaduna and Ibadan, finally reaching Lagos on 30 July 1929. They had crossed Africa with vehicles from east to west, and were the first people to have done so. As a logistical exercise, this was an extraordinary undertaking, as they had to plan all the places for fuel dumps in meticulous detail. The distance from Mombasa to Lagos is 5,545 miles, but they in fact travelled 13,282 miles. Considering that in many places there were no roads of any sort, and they never knew whether the planned fuel would be waiting where and when they needed it, it was extraordinary that they made it, apparently without even having a single puncture.

The film was dubbed 'the first African adventure film with sound'. I do not think this is quite true. It is more likely that it was a hybrid. An article in the *New York Times* of 20 September 1930 says that the 'informative and often highly exciting feature is accompanied by a Movietone lecture describing the various scenes'. Hoefler is alleged to have said that 'all the sounds of animals in the film were authentic, having been recorded as the camera was turned'.

Personally I would not describe the noise wildebeest make as being anything like the noise of a lion, as the commentary goes. They may well have recorded animal sounds while they were filming, but certainly not in sync with the camera. In the film the sounds bear no relation to the animals on screen. There is sound of a sort, but disconcertingly not in the right places, and much of it has clearly been faked in a studio.

On return to the US, Hoefler did not really know what to do with the 40,000 feet of footage and he hired Walter A Futter, a Hollywood producer, to put it all together. Futter's first decision was to 'flip' the whole expedition in the film, making the journey start in Lagos and finish in Mombasa. His reasoning was that the lions and other wildlife should be the climax of the film, and that as there were not many lions in Lagos, this was the most sensible way to structure the film. Futter clearly had no idea of African geography, so to anyone who knows the continent the locations are not in logical sequence, whether travelling east-west or west-east. While Hoefler had a lot of footage, Futter decided he needed more to link the scenes, and this was done in Westlake Village, California, with a full sound truck, grips, and a replica of the vehicle they had used in Africa. They also used back projection to insert Hoefler and Austin into many of the African shots.

Comparing this film with others of the same era, it was probably the most 'real' of all the 'adventure' films up to that time. The information on some of the animals, birds, and people is more accurate than that of all of its predecessors put together, except for the sound. This was presumably because Hoefler listened to the local knowledge of Mike Cottar, though there is a passage in the book where Hoefler asks Mike to identify a very fluffy animal with huge eyes in a tree near their Serengeti camp fire. This can only be a bushbaby, but for some reason the answer was 'a lemur', which is a totally different animal endemic to Madagascar. So much for scientific accuracy. But who in an American audience of the day would have pulled him up on it?

Martin and Osa Johnson

Martin Johnson is described by master biographer Pascal Imperator as 'an experienced showman who sometimes reworked the facts in order to increase the popularity of his films'. That description seems to fit the man over a period of thirty years. On his first overseas trip with Jack London, he met a film crew in the Solomon Islands in 1908, and helped them with some of the filming and processing. On his return he started on the slide show/lecture circuit, using other people's slides. It was not until 1914 in New York that he started filming for himself. In 1917 some investors from Boston gave him some money to return to the Solomon Islands, and he set off for a year with a Universal camera and his wife Osa. The trip resulted in their first silent film, called *Among the Cannibal Isles of the South Pacific*. On a subsequent trip to the same area, with better cameras, they filmed a head curing ceremony and misrepresented it as 'cannibalism'. They were then advised to try filming wildlife, as audiences no longer wanted to see pictures of 'savages', and went to Borneo to do this. The film *Jungle Adventures* was the result, from which it can be seen clearly that the animals were not in their natural environment. Hence it was seen as a travel film. The film was re-cut into twenty short films, all released between 1921 and 1922. It was in 1921 year that Martin and Osa met Carl Akeley, who persuaded them to go to Africa, and to concentrate on wildlife.

They formed a new company, Martin Johnson African Films, and arrived in Mombasa in 1921. They knew nothing of Africa, and very little about wildlife, though they had adopted a baby gibbon in Borneo two years before. The Johnsons hired Bud Cottar to help them, rented a house in Nairobi and set up a studio. Their first foray into the bush was to the Athi plains, following the trail of so many before them. By 1922 they were travelling further afield, to northern Kenya. Martin had been impressed by Paul Rainey's footage filmed at Laisamis, so they headed there and also visited Marsabit for the first time. At Laisamis, they built blinds so that they could get closer to the waterhole – these were constructed of brick with palm frond roofs, and stayed there for many years. Arthur Radclyffe Dugmore came upon the blinds in 1924 and remarked that the architecture left a lot to be desired, but he used them just the same. By early 1923, the Johnsons had 100,000 feet of exposed film, which they took back to the US. They released this as a silent film called *Trailing African Wild Animals*. The film was moderately successful, mainly because audiences liked the diminutive and feisty Osa who appeared on screen, and they took the film on the lecture circuit. Carl Akeley encouraged them to return to Africa, and get more wildlife footage as he thought that this would encourage donations to the American Museum of Natural History (AMNH), and specifically to its Africa Hall, which Akeley had been working on for so long. The Johnsons approached George Eastman for sponsorship, which was initially refused, but Akeley persuaded him to invest US$10,000. Another company was formed, in conjunction with the American Museum of Natural History: the Martin Johnson African Expedition Corporation, under a trust arrangement. Johnson's collateral was all his previous film and stills, which were to be used by AMNH for the museum, with the Johnsons retaining distribution rights during the couple's lifetimes.

The Johnsons sailed via London at the end of 1923, and arrived in Mombasa in January 1924. They planned to make three films in three years. This time they were better prepared, with eleven stills cameras and ten movie cameras, five of which were Akeley cameras. Moving in with the Percival family in Parklands, they again hired Bud Cottar who arranged a screening of *Trailing African Wild Animals* at Nairobi's Theatre Royal. They then set off for Mount Marsabit where they built a house, a laboratory, staff quarters, and blinds by the lakeside. By the end of 1925, they felt they had finished a film which at the time they called *Wanderings of an Elephant*. Martin felt that there was insufficient excitement in it, and Terry Ramsaye the editor agreed – then as now, American audiences wanted action. This changed Martin's way of filming, and he now concentrated on filming large animals charging, dangerous escapes, all the 'thrills' that the audiences of the time apparently wanted to see. Kevin Brownlow, in his book *The War, the West, and the Wilderness* states 'To the pure documentarian, Mr. and Mrs. Johnson are beyond the pale, they regarded Africa as a kind of special effects department. They were obsessed by adventure in the Theodore Roosevelt sense and aimed exclusively for thrills.... They had no scruples about authenticity.'

In May 1926 Carl Akeley, along with George Eastman and Dr Pomeroy of AMNH, again visited Kenya and Tanganyika on a museum collecting trip. Eastman shot five lions. While in the Grumeti area of the western Serengeti, they set up a 'lion hunt' with some Kipsigis warriors imported from Kenya, which Martin Johnson filmed from professional hunter Pat Ayre's vehicle. The whole sequence was set up, with vehicles driving the lions into the open, and more vehicles blocking the lions' escape, all this being justified as providing a 'permanent record' for the museum. None of them ever said anything about how it was done, and it was ultimately George Eastman himself who let the cat out of the bag in a privately printed diary of his trip. In September, Eastman returned to the US with 4,400 feet of Johnson footage, while the Johnsons stayed in the Serengeti with Akeley until he left for the Congo. They then returned to Nairobi, where Pomeroy had bought them a house in Muthaiga, before going back to Marsabit to close down the camp. They had been at Marsabit for more than three years, but certainly were nowhere near their objective of three completed films. In January 1927 they decided to climb Mount Kenya by the eastern (Chogoria) route, which nearly ended in disaster as most of the party were struck by altitude sickness and had to descend. Osa lost consciousness, and nearly died of pneumonia, but eventually recovered several weeks later. The Johnsons then sailed back to the US, arriving in New York in August 1927.

1927 was a year that brought huge changes. The film *The Jazz Singer* — with sound – suddenly tolled the final bell for silent films. For a year or two there were hybrid films, a mixture of silent and sound, but clearly the way forward for films was that they must have sound, sync sound. This problem affected the Johnsons' African footage, and in January 1928 two versions of the film *Simba* were released, one with sound and one without. I understand that the AMNH has five versions in their collection, so clearly it was reversioned many times. The version that I have is silent, with funereal organ music. Titles are printed over painted dioramas, and at the beginning there is the usual exaggerated blurb about 'tireless patience, endless courage, privation, perils, thirst and fevers' that the couple supposedly endured while making the film. Osa was credited as co-producer and cinematographer, and of course appeared on screen. Looking at the film now, one cannot help but feel uncomfortable. While some of the wildlife footage was moderately good for its time, the people footage was atrocious, showing all too clearly the patronising, racist attitudes in America at that time. The lion hunt sequence was hyped up by inappropriately placed footage of Lumbwa tribesmen, portrayed as priests, a king and his queen (the latter smoking a cigar), which was as totally inaccurate then as it would be now. The hunt itself has sixty-five seconds of warriors surrounding a male lion, followed by nineteen seconds of Al Klein's footage with a quite different lion filmed many years previously (which had been purchased by Pomeroy), followed finally by eighty-five seconds of yet another lion apparently charging straight at Osa, who 'shoots' it – which she did not.

The version of *Simba* with sound was successful, and in 1928 Martin Johnson released a book, *Safari*, which helped promote it more. This was followed by another book *Lion*, ghost-written by Fitzhugh Green, and a biography by Green called *Martin Johnson, Lion Hunter*, both released in 1929. The Johnsons were now superstars.

George Eastman asked the Johnsons to return to Africa with him in 1927, in order to collect an elephant and some white rhino. They went by boat to Cairo, took a train to Khartoum, then another boat to Kodok in Sudan, where professional hunter Philip Percival met them with vehicles. They drove into the Congo, then to Uganda where Eastman shot his rhino and an elephant before returning home via Sudan. The Johnsons continued to Garamba, and to the Ituri Forest where they had their first encounter with pygmies. They then returned to Nairobi, and on to the Serengeti with five boy scouts where they obtained 52,000 feet of footage of lions and the wildebeest migration. Back in the US in August 1928, this footage was released as a hybrid/silent short film called *Across the World with Mr and Mrs Martin Johnson*, as well as a lecture show entitled *3 Boy Scouts in Africa*, and another lecture show called *Adventuring Johnsons*.

The Johnsons then started planning a Congo film, and for this they hired a sound cameraman Richard Maedler and a separate sound man Lewis Tappan. Osa released a children's book, *Jungle Babies*, which came out in 1930, by which time the Johnsons and their crew were back in Nairobi. They moved into their house in Muthaiga briefly before setting off for the Serengeti, and then to northern Kenya. Also with them was DeWitt Sage, who had some African experience, having been in the Congo and the Virungas, and who spoke French. In June 1930, they travelled through Uganda to the Ituri Forest to film pygmies, then hippos on the Rutshuru river, and finally to the Virungas. They had no success filming gorillas, but did tidy up Carl Akeley's grave, to the fury of Akeley's second wife Mary Jobe. They travelled west of the Virungas where they captured two teenage gorillas and a younger one they called Snowball. They then returned to Nairobi, and filmed these animals in a compound in their Muthaiga garden. While one of the gorillas was recovering from hair loss caused by stress, they took short trips to Nakuru, Isiolo, and the Aberdares. They tried desperately to get a rhino to charge their truck, but failed time after time. Spending more time in Nairobi, the Johnsons became part of the social scene, when Osa's drinking binges became widely known. In July 1931 they returned to the US with the three gorillas, a cheetah called Bong, two chimpanzees called Teddy and Bits, two monkeys called Eleanor and Kimo. All these animals were cared for in the Central Park Zoo. Then followed another lecture tour, *Wonders of the Congo*, after which they were exhausted and moved to a hotel in New York where they stayed for five years.

In March 1932, George Eastman's bone marrow cancer worsened and he committed suicide. In July, the Johnson film *Congorilla*, with full sound, was premièred in New York. It was embarrassingly full of racial gags, certainly no improvement on their previous films.

The Johnsons then bought two amphibious aeroplanes, a twin-engined ten-seater and a single-engined five-seater. They painted one with zebra stripes, and the other with giraffe markings. The two planes were named Osa's Ark and Spirit of Africa. Both the Johnsons took flying lessons, but they never really flew. They sailed for Cape Town with the planes and two pilots on board, arriving at the end of January 1933. It took ten days to fly to Nairobi, where they moved back into their Muthaiga house. They asked Hugh Stanton (who had worked on the notorious *Trader Horn* film) to catch some animals for them, which they filmed in the confines of the enclosure or cage in their garden. These animals included baboons, a leopard, a cheetah, some warthog and a lion. They set up and filmed a fight between a warthog and a leopard, which was much criticised by the American Museum of Natural History, and when not doing this they flew to various locations. They were the first to fly to Central Island in Lake Turkana, then to the Lorian swamp, Garissa, and the Serengeti. Their trips became more ambitious, and they flew to Kisumu from where they took a commercial flying boat on a four-day trip to Cairo. They flew back to the Ituri Forest, then to Nanyuki where Raymond Hook had rescued four baby cheetahs on Mount Kenya. Their two colourful aeroplanes flew all over the region, and were well known and well photographed. Then Osa got sick, and so in June 1934 they sold the house and flew to London, thence by boat to New York. They had covered 60,000 miles in the planes, and had 160,000 feet of film.

In New York, Martin worked on putting together two films, a feature for Fox called *Baboona* and a silent lecture film called *Wings over Africa*. Martin was diagnosed with diabetes, a condition from which he had suffered for some years, and they sold their remaining animals to the St Louis Zoo. *Baboona* was released in New York in January 1935, and was hailed as 'the best the Johnsons have produced'. It contains a rhino spearing sequence, 'justified' because the rhino had been killing Maasai cattle (which would never happen), and the set up sequence of a leopard/warthog fight, but there was a marked reduction in the racial slurs and gags that typified their earlier films. In places it is clear that their sound recordist was not present, with totally fake animal sounds in the set-up shots of baboons, monkeys and cheetah. Did people really believe that 'cheetah, leopard and hyena were attacking the monkeys from all sides'? There are shots of animals filmed from the air, most of which are running away. Martin's commentary notes that 'the higher we flew, the more scared was the game', and states that the animals were less frightened if the noisy aeroplanes were flying lower. There are aerial shots of small volcanic craters which Martin states authoritatively were caused by meteors.

In the same year, Martin released another book *Over African Jungles* about their aerial adventures. By August, they were off again, this time back to Borneo by ship, carrying the smaller plane, renamed Spirit of Africa and Borneo. They set up camp and sent people out to capture animals, which they again filmed in a studio cage. The gentle orang utans, which were almost unknown to Western cinema audiences, were perceived as 'terrorising the natives', and the footage is deeply offensive for its ignorance and inaccuracy. They sailed back to New York, where Martin cut the films *Adventuring through Borneo* and *Jungle Depths of Borneo*, as well as a commercial film for 20th Century Fox titled simply *Borneo*. Things were going well, until 12 January 1937 when both Johnsons were on a commercial flight that crashed. Both were injured, and Martin lapsed into a coma and died. Osa spent some time in a wheelchair, but recovered fully. Clark Getts, who had been in charge of managing the Johnsons' lecture tours, took over

Osa's financial affairs and by August was the new man in her life. Based on her knowledge of Africa, Getts arranged for Osa to be hired as a consultant for Zanuck's film *Stanley and Livingstone*, and the pair then sailed to London and took the flying boat to Kenya.

Borneo opened in New York in September 1937, and was very successful. When Osa and Getts returned in November, she immediately went on a lecture tour promoting the *Borneo* films. She tried to sue the airline over the crash that had killed Martin, but lost. She then started planning a film on Martin's life, and put together a new lecture tour called *Jungles Calling*. By 1938, encouraged by Getts, she had become a glamorous lady, and was voted one of the 'best dressed women' in America. She launched her own fashion range of designer clothes, followed by a range of toy animals, all astutely marketed by Getts. She hired a ghost-writer, Winifred Dunn, to write a biography of her and Martin's life. *I Married Adventure* was published in May 1940, and became a best seller. The film of the same title premièred in September in New York and although it was panned by critics, it was nevertheless successful. *I Married Adventure* is a hotchpotch of old footage, from the Solomon Islands, Kenya, Uganda, Tanzania, Congo, Egypt, and Borneo, cobbled together with titles such as 'the greatest pictures ever taken'. Osa and Getts married secretly in April 1940, and a public wedding followed in February 1941. A second book, *Four Years in Paradise*, was published in November 1941, and a new lecture tour *African Paradise* began. This has also been released as a film (silent with sound overlay) following the more recent discovery of the original film by the Martin & Osa Johnson Museum in Kansas. This is a re-work of footage that had appeared in both *Simba* and *Baboona*, and a few obvious out-takes, and as such is fairly incoherent. Osa also turned some of the children's stories she had written into books. She sold some footage to William Cayton, who produced fifty-two fifteen-minute programmes, collectively shown under the title *Jungle*. She was successful, but she was not happy, and she started drinking again. Getts put her into a psychiatric hospital in 1944, and she never went back to him. After a bitter legal battle, they were divorced in 1949.

But the Johnson machine went on turning. In 1950, twenty-six half-hour programmes were released under the title *Osa Johnson's Big Game Hunt*. *Congorilla* and *Borneo* were released again. Osa's lawyer John Crane moved in with her, but most people thought that he was quite wrong for her. In 1951, Bud Cottar's daughter Myrtle (who infamously had left all Charles Cottar's film on a bus) visited Osa in Park Avenue. They had a heated argument about the way gerenuks drink (or indeed whether they drink at all), revealing Osa's very sketchy knowledge of animal behaviour. Osa's life at this stage was not good – she had coronary artery problems, and was in financial difficulty. She suffered a heart attack on 7 January 1953 at the age of 58, and was buried five days later.

Whatever may be said about the quality of their films, and their lack of genuine wildlife knowledge, the Johnsons were significant in the history of film. They were the first couple to travel and make films together, with Osa becoming the first female on-screen presenter. Their footage was recycled in a way that has never been matched, and they rode the wave of change from silent films and lecture tours to full-sound cinema productions.

Trader Horn

MGM's *Trader Horn* was taken from a book by Ethelreda Lewis, published in 1927, allegedly based on some of the life (on the Ogowe River in Gabon) of one Alfred Aloysius 'Wish' Smith, who called himself Trader Horn. He was apparently born in Scotland, raised in Lancashire in northern England, and had at times been a sailor, a detective, an ivory hunter, a cowboy and a river pilot. Presented as 'a true story', if somewhat embellished, the book was a non-fiction best seller in 1927–8. Billed as 'the first feature film – with sound' to be filmed on location, the film was released in 1931. Sound was still a new thing, and it did not help that the sound truck fell overboard in Mombasa harbour. In addition, the sound recordist Andy Anderson became progressively deafer as the shoot went on, which was blamed on liberal doses of quinine. Director W.S. (Woody) van Dyke and his team spent seven months filming in Kenya, Uganda, Tanzania and the Ituri Forest in Congo. The main characters were played by Harry Carey and Edwina Booth (whose real name was Constance Woodruff), both former silent-movie stars. Her choice of stage name presumably had something to do with one Edwin Booth, who was some time elocution teacher to Alfred Aloysius Smith. They hired two top professional hunters in Kenya, W. ('Dicker') Dickinson and A.S. Waller, and two assistants Hugh Stanton and Jim Barnes, to run the entire expedition and take care of the 90 tons of equipment.

Van Dyke was born in California in 1889, and is said to have started a stage career at the age of three – his mother was an actress. Before getting into movies, he was at times a gold miner, a waiter, a grocery clerk, a salesman, a train driver and, some say, a mercenary in Mexico. He directed his first film in 1917, and through the 1920s worked mainly on westerns, earning himself a reputation for delivering films on time and within budget. Some considered his methods to be slapdash, but 'one take Woody' took on the challenge of a long shoot in Africa with no complaint, and the film was nominated for a best picture Oscar.

He published a tongue-in-cheek and not entirely accurate account of this adventure, called *Horning into Africa*, which revealed a cynical respect for all things African, and a wry sense of humour. Few copies remain, and the book cannot be taken as a serious contribution to history, but it caused amusement at the time. In the book, there is a photo of a local actor called Mutia, who played the role of Horn's gun bearer Rencharo. The caption reads 'Mutia never did understand what it was all about, he just did what the crazy white man told him, and nearly stole the picture'. Van Dyke went on to higher things until he committed suicide in 1943. Harry Carey progressed to become an Oscar winning actor, but Edwina Booth never appeared in another film. It was said that she had contracted an unknown tropical disease while shooting *Trader Horn* and was bedridden for years, though it is more likely that she had a nervous breakdown. She became a Mormon and died in the 1970s at the age of eighty-six.

The storyline is pure jungle fiction, in fact so much so that it is said that Edgar Rice Burroughs based his first Tarzan film on its theme (*Tarzan the Ape Man*, 1932, also directed by Van Dyke). That said, there are a lot of wild animals, some apparently filmed in almost natural conditions with a Carl Akeley camera, although some sequences were certainly 'set up' with captive animals. One particular sequence shows four big, black maned lions fighting to the death. This behaviour is most unlikely to happen in the wild, and the animals were probably starved and filmed in a small enclosure with a piece of meat thrown in to encourage a fight. According to Greg Mitman, MGM complained that there was not enough carnage in the footage, and they commissioned a second unit to go to Mexico to stage some set-ups with animals from a zoo, some of which were obviously regarded as dispensable. The locations, according to the credits, were Kenya, Tanganyika, Uganda, Congo and part of the Sudan. How then did the southern African species of zebra, some gemsbok, lechwe and springbok get into the picture, in scenes that – judging from the vegetation – could not possibly have been filmed anywhere else other than in South Africa?

I mention *Trader Horn*, not because it was in any way a 'wildlife' movie, but because it was the first in a series of films that moved the trend away from the 'explorer' kind of film. The end was in sight for Martin and Osa Johnson creeping up on 'unsuspecting' animals, he with a camera and she with a rifle. The Hollywood factor had come to Africa, and while the stories may have been spurious, the animals were certainly there – not to be collected for some distant museum, but to appear on screen in their own right with a semi-coherent dialogue that gave them a little dignity. It would still be a few years, however, before scientists and nature lovers became involved in wildlife filming, giving proper credence to their subjects.

The worldwide recession and the Second World War interrupted the progress of this changing scenario, and it was not until the late 1940s and early 1950s that yet another variation of the genre developed.

The Queeny Expedition (1949–50)

From the very early days, the American Museum of Natural History (AMNH) organised expeditions to Africa, frequently to collect animals for the Museum's display, and also to record the local people whose costumes and dances held a fascination for the Americans of the day. Many of these expeditions travelled through Kenya in order to get to Tanzania, Sudan, Ethiopia, Uganda and Congo, or other nearby countries. Films from these expeditions are in the museum's library.

There were many of these trips, including those of Carl Akeley in 1921–2, William James Morden in 1922 and 1924, and again in 1947 and 1956, Martin and Osa Johnson in 1924 and 1928, George Eastman with Pomeroy and Akeley in 1926, William Campbell in 1938, Harry Snyder also in 1938, the Central African Expedition in 1948 led by James L Clark, Edgar Monsanto Queeny in 1949–50 and again in 1952, David and Barbara Lowry in 1959, and Gardner and Clare Stout in 1972.

Edgar Queeny was chairman of the Monsanto chemical company, a naturalist and filmmaker, and a trustee of the AMNH from 1949–68. On his first trip to East Africa at the end of 1949, he set off on safari from the Norfolk hotel with John Williams, the ornithologist from the Coryndon Museum in Nairobi (now called National Museum of Kenya), and two professional hunters, Donald Ker of Ker & Downey Safaris, and Tony Dyer. Queeny and his cameraman Dick Bishop had already proved themselves to be experts on birds, having won an award for a film on ducks in Arkansas called *Prairie Wings*. They started in the Maasai Mara, where they filmed Maasai Ndorobo people (named as Koaigige Ole Sene, Sabartwa Ole Roisa and Jimgwa Ole Naisho) interacting with a honeyguide. This is a bird that calls people and leads them to a bees' nest. The people then cut open the nest and take most of the honey, leaving behind a small portion as a 'reward' for the bird. I believe that this is the first film that documented this mutually beneficial relationship between birds and man. The subject has been filmed several times since, most recently in 2009 by the BBC Natural History Unit for their series *Human Planet*. Queeny's 16mm colour film *Wandorobo* is short (twenty-nine minutes), and also includes the same Ndorobo people hunting a topi with poisoned arrows. The film was also reversioned as part of the CBS/AMNH *Adventure* television series, aired in 1954 with the title *Wild Birds and Man*. The trip's purpose was also to collect birds, and Tony Dyer found a new species of Greenbul in the Kakamega forest. Having John Williams on the expedition also paid off, as they doubled the world's collection of rare swifts.

Queeny's first trip also took him into Wakamba country, where he made a fictional film, *Wakamba*, of which the museum directors did not approve, although there was a lot of good wildlife footage in it. He then took the expedition to the Sudan and came back with several films on the Dinka and Madi people.

In 1952, Queeny returned with footage of his previous trip to show to the Maasai people and, with their agreement, made a longer film (two hours) called *Maasailand* which is described as a 'rich ethnographic portrait' of Maasai warriors. This includes the spearing of two lions, but in addition there is a lot of natural wildlife footage. Tony Dyer was relegated to the role of sound recordist, trained by Jack Clink, and shot 42,000 feet of synch film, with equipment that he says weighed 350 pounds.

At 2¹/₂ years

At 3 years

My early years

At 5 years

At 9 years

The balloonagraph's first flight in Kenya, 1909. *Courtesy of Sue Deverell*

Top: The 'Trader Horn' crew, 1931, Woody Van Dyke is at the back, standing centre, Chief cameraman Clyde de Vinna centre with pipe, Standing right, hunter AS Waller, sitting left hunter Dicker Dickinson.
Courtesy AS Waller collection and Monty Brown

Below: Harry Carey, star of 'Trader Horn' with hunter AS Waller.
Courtesy AS Waller collection and Monty Brown

Top: 1. Edwina Booth with hunter AS Waller. *Courtesy AS Waller collection and Monty Brown*

Below: Ava Gardner, suitably dressed, with one of Carr Hartley's elephants during the making of 'Mogambo'. *Courtesy Monty Brown*

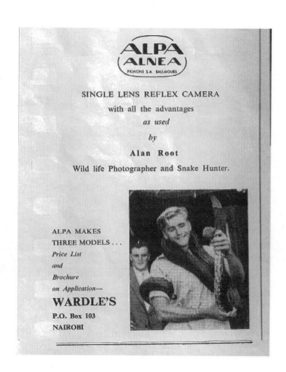

Top: A camera advertisement, 1958

Below: George Adamson and Christian the lion. *Courtesy Simon Trevor*

Top: A reluctant mermaid. *Courtesy Carr Hartley collection*

Below: Simon Trevor filming lions at Kora. *Courtesy Simon Trevor*

Armand and Michaela Denis

'A nature film must be true to nature; let it be entertaining by all means, and further it is a great advantage if it is also instructive, which does not mean that it need be tedious.' – Joseph Delmont, 1925.

Armand Denis was a one-off, and there is no doubt in my mind that he deserves a place in film history. It took him a while to 'find' Africa, but once he had done that, he was hooked. Born in Belgium, his early interest in nature started at three years old when he started breeding flies in a matchbox. He learned the rudiments of photography and enlisted at the beginning of the First World War. After escaping the Germans in the Netherlands, he went to England, and got a job in a chemistry lab before joining the Royal Air Force (RAF) as a chemist working on lubricating oils. This led to him eventually studying chemistry at the University of Oxford. At this time he was questioning religion, and to get things straight in his mind he joined a monastery in Italy. Science won, and he joined an engineering company and then a school of mining. He won a fellowship in the US, and joined a laboratory as a research chemist. He started collecting reptiles, including, illegally, a Galapagos tortoise which travelled the world with him until he eventually left it in Bali. In 1926 he became interested in radio, and designed a way of adjusting the volume, which he patented.

Royalties from this invention enabled him to buy two wooden De Brie cameras, a tripod and a lens, and he set off to the South Seas to make his first film in 1931. He collected various monkeys, and filmed everything he saw. This eventually resulted in the film *Goona Goona* although the film was damaged by sea water and appeared to be unusable. When he got it back to the US, he went to the Eastman studio for help, and while there found a way to save it by inventing an automatic printer. Eastman gave him US$5,000 for this, and Armand joined a laboratory to try and develop a way of recording sound on film. Still the avid collector, he collected snakes, and made a film on them for Eastman. While finishing *Goona Goona* with Eastman, he learned editing, and then sold the film to a distributor for US$35,000. He also met Martin and Osa Johnson.

An agent put him in touch with Frank Buck, who had made a film called *Bring 'em Back Alive* and wanted to do a sequel. Armand reluctantly directed the sequel, called *Wild Cargo*, but he and Buck disagreed on a daily basis, and it was not a happy experience for him. Armand said 'There was no need to fake or think up impossible adventures as he (Buck) did. The truth was far more exciting'.

In 1935, Armand organised his first filming trip to Africa. He persuaded Chrysler to donate two trucks in exchange for a short film, and Texaco donated fuel. He and his somewhat formidable first wife Leila, a relative of Theodore Roosevelt, set off with Akeley cameras and some sound equipment that Armand had designed. In all they had 16 tons of equipment and they sailed to Antwerp where they met the Belgian king. The king wanted a film made about the Albert National Park, and after crossing the Sahara they spent six months filming in the Congo. They then drove east to Kenya's coast, and back to Nigeria, across the Sahara again to Europe. The film for Chrysler was called *Wheels Across Africa*, and his own film, *Dark Rapture*. The latter featured Watutsi circumcision ceremonies, a lot of 'tribal' music, and the trained elephants of the Congo. There was a lot of footage of pygmies, and of the famous four-tusked elephant (whose skull now resides in the Explorers' Club in New York). Leila wrote the scripts for both films. They returned to the US, and spent many months editing.

In 1939, Armand and Leila set off on another expedition to Burma, China and Tibet. They went to Nepal as war broke out and then had to leave before planned. They sailed to Mombasa where they met professional hunter and naturalist Al Klein who took them to Ngorongoro crater to film lions for three weeks. But the war made filming difficult, and they returned to the US. Armand then set up a chimpanzee research station in Florida, and gave up filmmaking for the duration of the war. In 1944, he set off to Brazzaville in an attempt to collect some lowland gorillas for his primate research station, but this ended in disaster. Many were killed during capture, and all the rest (thirty) died of some unknown human disease. He had filmed the captures, and put his precious footage on a ship to America. The ship sank and he lost it all. He then abandoned his chimpanzees, and sent them all to an ape farm. The war was over, but everything was in short supply and it took him a while to assemble another package of equipment. In 1946 he was ready for another African trip, and he returned to the Congo where he attempted to collect more gorillas. He filmed gorillas, elephants, pygmies, and okapi being caught in traps, before driving to Kenya. Here he was shocked to find that the amount of game was a fraction of that which he had seen on his previous visits. He was told it had all been shot in order to feed both troops and prisoners of war. He also noted that forests had been destroyed, and was horrified. He realised that film was an important way of educating people about wildlife, and decided to make another film.

With Lewis Cotlow, he embarked on *Savage Splendour*, working with veterinarian Toni Haarthoorn. In the film, animals are captured by lasso rather than killed. During this trip he filmed at Mzima Springs, and was the first to film hippos underwater. He adapted a galvanised water tank into a kind of coffin in order to make this work. This technique (with some improvements) was subsequently used by Al and Elma Milotte in Disney's *True Life Adventure* film *The African Lion*; by Simon Trevor in *The Last Safari*, by Alan Root in his film *Mzima, Portrait of a Spring*; and more recently by Mark Deeble and Victoria Stone in their film *Mzima, Haunt of the River Horse*.

Armand returned to the US to edit *Savage Splendour* and it was released in 1949, after he had sued Lewis Cotlow who had claimed it as his film. He and Leila separated, and he met fashion designer Michaela Holdsworth at a party. He then planned a trip to South America to film the 'native Indians'. This is where he met up with Michaela again, and they were married high in the Andes at Potosi.

In 1950 Armand was invited by MGM to be technical adviser on the feature film *King Solomon's Mines*, and Michaela was contracted to double for actress Deborah Kerr. They spent six months working on this, and at the end Armand took his name off the credits. He and Michaela had decided that Kenya was the place they wanted to settle, and they bought a plot in the Langata suburb of Nairobi. They then set off on another African trip called *Below the Sahara*, which took them back to the pygmies in the Congo, and to Namibia and South Africa. Their cameraman on this trip was Tom Stobart, who shot 50,000 feet of film in eighteen months. They next planned three short films, two in Australia and one in New Guinea. In Australia they met Des Bartlett, who filmed all three. These were edited by Armand in Cuba, before they tried to sell them in America. The Americans wanted to merge all three films into one, so Armand took them to the UK where Ealing Studios accepted all three as separate films. They were screened in England very successfully, and Armand and Michaela appeared on a television chat-show to promote them. This resulted in a television contract that was to last over a decade, first for *Filming Wild Animals* and then *On Safari*. The couple moved to Kenya permanently, built their house, collected more and more pets, and that was just the beginning.

Armand Denis, in his autobiography, made it sound as if he had done all the filming himself. This is not true, as he always had an assistant who actually operated the camera, but he gave them little or no credit. In South America in 1948, it was a man called Bodo. In Mexico it was Niels Halbertsma. In *Wheels Across Africa* it was Leroy Phelps. In the Congo it was Duncan. In Asia it was Grant Wolfkill. In French Equatorial Africa, filming gorillas and okapi, it was someone called Robert (possibly Robert Carmet, who also filmed in New Guinea). In *Below the Sahara* it was Tom Stobart. For the three films that effectively launched his television career with the BBC, it was Des Bartlett. There may have been others, but Armand was very careful not to let them take any of his limelight. Tom Stobart left as Des Bartlett joined, and Tom filmed the successful Everest ascent of 1952 with Sir Edmund Hillary.

Des Bartlett joined Armand Denis in 1952 and stayed with him, filming all over the world until 1965 when Armand became ill with Parkinson's disease and the company folded, at which time Des joined Survival.

During all the time that Des Bartlett was with Armand Denis, Armand only filmed one sequence himself. This was one minute and fifteen seconds of a sunbirds' nest, hanging from the ceiling of a Kenyan verandah. Armand was seated in a chair underneath the nest. I have a copy of this momentous footage. Perhaps one should have grudging admiration for the man for creating this image of himself as chief cameraman, and having the world believe him.

Whatever his limitations as a cameraman, Armand Denis, with his glamorous on-screen wife Michaela, started something new. He loved nature, he loved travel and he was fascinated by indigenous people in all the places he visited. As with most presenters, he had an ego, but he also had foresight. Who else in the 1940s even considered using the medium of film as an educational tool to protect wildlife and the environment? And even though early television was only in black and white, Armand foresaw that one day it would be in colour. So his films were shot in colour, to be ready for the big day when technology caught up with his predictions – in this alone, he was ahead of his time, and it paid off. The public loved the programmes, and a whole new audience was created. *Filming Wild Animals* ran for three years, and *On Safari* ran for ten. In the early 1950s television programmes on the BBC tended to be studio-based such as *Look* with Peter Scott, and even David Attenborough's *Zoo Quest* had part of each programme in the studio.

The Armand Denis programmes, however, were all filmed on location, with Armand driving badly and far too fast across the savannahs of Africa, or in New Guinea, or in South America or Australia. Many of the animals were tame, as both Armand and Michaela loved having a houseful of pets of all kinds, at one time over 130 of them – but at least they admitted this fact, as viewers were introduced to Minnie the Mongoose, Chui the Leopard, and many others. Charlie and Brigitte the chimpanzees, Hoppy the African spring hare, Numa and Puss the two servals, and Gilbert the baboon became familiar friends to countless television viewers, along with Simba Kali the caracal, Bertram the bushbaby, Nugu the Colobus monkey, Marilyn the vervet, and Monsieur Robert the bat-eared fox. There was a spotted hyena called Stinky that Simon Trevor rescued from a culvert, but he was constantly stealing things and was not one of their favourites. Michaela does not mention him in her books, and I wondered why until Simon explained to me that Stinky had once disrobed Michaela in the presence of guests. Stinky's best friend was a young warthog called Piggy, who used to sleep with Des and Jen's daughter Julie.

Others included a green pigeon called Sweetie Pie, a dikdik called Dickie, two duikers called Baba and Billy, Horrie the Ground Hornbill, Voodoo the vulture, Bushy the bushbuck, Little Tich the bushbaby and one of Alan Root's bongos called Karen. Their pets were not all African animals, with Bruni the sunbear, Lily the spectacled langur, a handsome lion-tailed macaque, a Sulphur-crested Cockatoo called Squawky and a South American giant anteater all apparently living in harmony in the Denises' Langata home. Often they would load all these creatures into travelling cages and take them to Crescent Island, Lake Naivasha where they filmed them 'behaving normally'. Jen Bartlett's brother Terry was sometimes called in to help handle the animals on these trips to the lake. Nowadays, shots of Gilbert choosing between seven glasses of orange juice may seem absurd, but at the time it was popular and audiences got to see the animals in close-up. As well as learning about the exotic pets, a new generation of viewers was able to watch at last wildlife behaving non-defensively in almost natural habitat. There were no guns, no mock charges, no horrendous Maasai lion hunts that had been the norm in films prior to 1940.

On Safari might have been a bit syrupy, with Michaela always having every hair in place and her lipstick to hand, and Armand's and her commentaries were rather stilted – but the wildlife footage was excellent. Cameras had improved beyond recognition, and a new breed of wildlife cameramen were beginning to make their mark.

Al and Elma Milotte

Another extraordinary husband and wife team were Alfred and Elma Milotte, from Alaska, who started with a small photographic studio in Seattle and ended up winning eight Oscars for Disney's *True Life Adventures* in the 1950s. Their film *The African Lion* was nearly three years in the making, during which time they shot 300,000 feet of 35mm film. They had a specially adapted Dodge power wagon, complete with bunks, kitchen, bathroom, and darkroom so that they were self contained. A high level hide on the roof enabled them to get high angle shots, and there was a hole in the floor so that Al could get to ground level. The vehicle was incredibly heavy as a result of all these extraneous fittings, and Elma estimated the fuel consumption at two miles to the gallon. The Milottes worked as a team, with Al on camera and Elma doing the sound.

The Milottes started filming in the Kruger National Park in South Africa in 1952, but then decided to move to the Serengeti where there were more animals. Much of the footage was filmed in Tanzania, but they also spent time in Kenya. Whether they knew Armand and Michaela Denis I cannot say for certain, but I suspect that they must have run into each other. They certainly worked at Mzima Springs, and had a coffin with a glass window made in Nairobi to enable them to film hippos underwater, almost identical in design to that used by Armand for his 1949 film *Savage Splendour*. They managed to shoot barbels cleaning a hippo's teeth, so clearly the hippo was not stressed by their presence.

While they were at Mzima, the then Governor of Kenya went to visit them, with a view to assessing Mzima as a possible source of water for the town of Mombasa. The Milottes convinced him that the water was so full of hippo dung that it was not suitable, and claimed that in so doing they had 'saved Mzima'. The water supply was taken from another area close by, but the main spring was left alone. They also visited Amboseli, and managed to get a fleeting shot of the famous rhino, Gertie, and her calf, who had featured in an *On Safari* programme called *The search for Gertie*.

As a film, *African Lion* is visually magnificent – with high quality images and some excellent sequences. As was the case with Disney films of the time, there is no real story, and much of the film is a shopping list of other African animals, put together by editor Norman Palmer. The commentary is in a somewhat banal, documentary style with some major inaccuracies and several instances of blatant anthropomorphism. A large bull elephant is described as being 'a hundred to two hundred years old', a Kori Bustard is described as a 'greater' bustard, and watching a male lion we are told 'the royal spouse rests on his laurels and wonders what's holding up lunch'. Paul Smith's music is used alongside a sequence of a baby elephant chasing egrets. There is a sequence of a courser's courtship dance which I have never seen anywhere else, a wonderful study of a jacana cleaning out the ears of a hippo, and some stunning shots of storks in a swarm of locusts.

The Milottes had an obvious understanding of nature, and managed to get close to their subjects. In an interview in 1985, Elma said she was convinced that the animals did not view them as a threat, but understood that the Milottes meant them no harm. She also explained that they never felt they were working for the Disney Corporation, but solely for their friend Walt, so they did not feel under pressure in any way.

As a Disney *True Life Adventure*, *The African Lion* is one of the best, certainly from the point of view of the camerawork. Walt Disney himself described Al Milotte as 'the greatest nature photographer in the world'. Of course the publicity was hyped up as a 'primitive pageant of nature's Africa', 'a story as big as Africa itself', '3 danger-filled years in the making', 'here comes nature's greatest drama'. It was billed as 'unstaged', 'unrehearsed' and 'unbelievable'. Yet *The African Lion* was the only *True Life Adventure* that was filmed in Africa.

Born Free (film and television series), Joy and George Adamson

A series of films and television programmes, and the eventual creation of several conservation organisations, came about through one of the most extraordinarily mismatched couples in the country's history, and there have been a few. They were George Adamson, essentially a solitary character, game warden and naturalist, and his somewhat difficult Austrian wife Joy.

George was first a hunter, and then a temporary game warden in northern Kenya before the outbreak of the Second World War when he joined military intelligence until returning to the Game Department in 1942. Joy arrived in Kenya in 1937, and married botanist Peter Bally a year later. For a couple of months in 1940, she was interned as an enemy alien, but this was short term and in 1941 she had an exhibition of flower paintings. She and George met in Garissa at Christmas 1942, and they were married in Nairobi in January 1944. She attended the Slade School of Art in London, and received a medal for her flower paintings. In 1948 she started painting people, trying to capture traditional dress – eventually these paintings formed the basis of a book *People of Kenya*, released much later in 1967. The original paintings are hanging in the National Museum in Nairobi, and some are at State House.

In January 1956, George was working for the Game Department when he shot a lioness. Too late, he realised that she had three cubs, and he rescued these and took them back to Joy. Two of them were sent to the Rotterdam zoo, but one remained – the famous Elsa. Thus began a consuming obsession that was to result in books, films, lectures, and considerable fame and success for Joy. Elsa became Joy's surrogate child, her whole reason for living. She was not exactly the kind of person filled with a caring spirit, as many people will testify: she treated people abominably and was well known for being racist, arrogant, abrupt and rude. She decided to 'raise' Elsa, and to reintroduce her to the wild when she was big enough to fend for herself. That this happened was largely due to George, who had far more empathy with nature and who constantly advised his wife how to care for the cub.

Elsa became part of the family, going on trips to Turkana and the coast with the Adamsons, and becoming increasingly famous. Everyone knows the story – she went off into the wild, found a boyfriend, and brought her first litter of cubs back to the Adamsons for inspection. Whether all this did anything for conservation has been questioned many times. The truth is that the Adamsons did a lot for Elsa, and for other individual lions such as Boy, Girl, and Christian (the likeable lion from Harrods), but they did not go as far as to offer the same kind of sanctuary or indeed any kind of protection for other lions, and in fact George shot 'wild' lions in considerable numbers. Joy's relationship with Elsa made an already difficult marriage even more problematic, and George was happiest when they were separated by as many miles of African bush as possible. Joy was murdered, allegedly by one of her former staff in Shaba, and George was mown down by bandits' AK47s in Meru. His camp at Kora has been maintained, and their house at Naivasha, Elsamere, is now a conservation centre and small hotel.

Joy's book *Born Free* was published in 1960, and sold several million copies. It was followed by *Living Free* in 1961 and *Forever Free* in 1962. The feature film *Born Free*, starring Virginia McKenna and Bill Travers, was filmed in 1964–5 and released in 1966 with a Royal première at which function Joy turned up wearing the same dress as Her Majesty the Queen. Next came *Living Free* in 1972, with Susan Hampshire and Nigel Davenport playing the lead roles, filmed by Jack Couffer. Then followed the television series, starring Gary Collins and Diana Muldaur in 1976, also filmed by Jack Couffer. The public lapped up the films. Joy went on to the lecture circuit, with a series of lecture films: *Elsa and her Cubs* by Benchmark Films, *Born Free* by Collins and the Elsa Trust, *Penny the Leopard* by LWT and finally some uncut silent footage of *Pippa the Cheetah*. In 1960 David Attenborough passed through Kenya briefly and went to meet Elsa not long before she died – this resulted in a black and white programme called *Elsa the Lioness*.

Bill Travers and Virginia McKenna were hooked, and they returned to make another film, *The Lions are Free*, which was the story of the return to the wild of the lions that had been used in the film *Born Free*. A couple of years later they starred in *An Elephant called Slowly*, featuring Daphne Sheldrick's orphaned elephants. The elephant was actually called Pole Pole, which is Kiswahili for 'slowly'. Back in London Bill and Virginia heard about Christian, a young lion who had been rescued from Harrods and was living in a furniture showroom in Chelsea with his rescuers John Rendall and Ace Bourke. They undertook to persuade George Adamson to agree to take Christian and release him back into the wild in the Kora National Park in Kenya. This resulted in a film called *Lion at World's End*, produced by Beckmann Communications in 1971, a book of the same name, and another film called *Christian the Lion* in 1972. An update of this story was produced in 2009 by Blink Films. Several other documentaries were made as the Adamson fan base grew:

The Story of Joy Adamson in 1980, directed and produced by Dick Thomsett and narrated by Derek Jones; *Lord of the Lions* about George and produced by Yorkshire Television; *George Adamson, Father of the Lions* produced by Kenya Broadcasting Corporation; and, later, *Reputations, the Joy Adamson Story* by the BBC in 1996. In 1998, the feature film *To Walk with Lions* was made, starring Richard Harris.

Now, fifty years since *Born Free* was written, a rash of 'George and Joy Adamson/Elsa revisited' films are being made. The impact of a single lioness, due to the marketing skills of an exceptional publisher, and an acerbic Austrian woman, was enormous.

Thomas Carr Hartley

Thomas Carr Hartley was my uncle in law, a larger than life character who had come to Kenya from South Africa in the early 1920s. He borrowed money from Dr J.R. Gregory and purchased a farm at Rumuruti, which he leased out, not moving to live there himself until

1934. He was employed culling crop-raiding elephants in the Embu/ Meru area for some years, but was then asked to catch a cheetah for the Shah of Dinga Por. It is thought that this started him on collecting animals, and his Rumuruti farm became known for the large collection that he amassed. Carr, his animals, and indeed his family, were involved in no less than fifty-eight films, but he only made one film himself with his brother in law Tom Mann, who wrote the script and directed.

This was extraordinarily ambitious for the time (1958), and the film was called *The Reluctant Mermaid*. Loosely, the story involved two young scientists (played by Ian Pritchard and Gina White) who were searching for a dugong, to obtain blood samples for research purposes. They chartered a dhow and set out to hunt for dugongs, which were more plentiful than they are today. It took six weeks before they caught their first dugong at Kynoli, a five-foot long female (whom they named Scylla), which they wrapped in wet blankets and rushed to the (salt water) swimming pool at the Eden Roc Hotel in Malindi. The next day they caught a second dugong, this time a ten-foot female, named Electra. At that time, there were no dugongs in captivity, and many people warned that it would be impossible to make a film about them, for they would surely die. But for five days these animals were filmed in the pool, before being safely released back into the ocean near Casuarina Point on 14 October 1958.

It is amazing that the team managed to make this film – not only because no one had ever caught dugongs before, but also because underwater filming was still in its infancy. Jacques Cousteau and Hans Hass were just beginning, and so for cameraman Freddie Ford and his assistant Jim Marshall, this was ground-breaking stuff. As well as the swimming pool footage of the dugongs, they also filmed a two-ton manta ray in the open sea, and the capture of a turtle by means of a remora (sucker fish).

Sadly the film was never shown to the public due, it is said, to some legality where it was claimed that Carr Hartley Film Productions were not members of a union. The family has searched the world for a copy, but to date have been unsuccessful.

Before the dugong film, Carr and his son Mike were involved in the filming of *Zanzabuku* (also known as *Dangerous Safari*) which was released in 1956. The filmmaker Lewis Cotlow (who had worked with Armand Denis on *Savage Splendour* in 1949), was on his third trip to Africa and filmed many of Carr's animals. He also spent time in Tsavo with Carr's brother Lionel (my father in law), who was known as Rhino Hartley for calling wild rhinos to him. Cotlow also filmed in Tanzania, using animals collected by August Kuenzler and his assistant Pellegrini, and relied heavily on safari expert Alan Tarlton when he needed snakes. Clearly he was not willing to spend time filming animals in the wild, and indeed seemed very blasé on the subject:

> *I had been able to kill bait for lions, provoke a rhino into a charge, startle a herd of impala into hasty flight, frighten buffalo or zebra into a stampede – in other words, annoy or scare the animals enough to provide action for my camera… Five times we organised animal stampedes and four times we failed to film them satisfactorily.*

Clearly, Lewis Cotlow would not be considered a credible wildlife filmmaker today.

Carr Hartley's son Mike, brought up like many Kenya kids with wild animals, joined the film world as a child star in *Zanzabuku* (or *Dangerous Safari*). He then took the lead in a series called *Jungle Boy* produced by Kenya Productions Ltd in Nairobi alongside Gross-Krasne Inc and Phoenix Productions from Hollywood, which was aired on British television as well as in the US. At the same time George Breakston produced thirty-nine half-hour episodes of *African Patrol* starring John Bentley as a policeman sorting out all sorts of problems, often involving incidents involving hunters and clients on safari, using Carr's animals. Breakston also produced *Escape in the Sun*, in which Alan Tarlton (founder of Newland and Tarlton, the safari company) featured as a professional hunter.

Other films in which Carr's animals appeared were the Hollywood features of the 1950s – *Mogambo, King Solomon's Mines, Where no Vultures Fly, Munchausen in Africa, Safari, Kamata Faru, Hatari, The Snows of*

Kilimanjaro, Men Against the Sun, Not so Dark Africa, Animals in Africa and more. His favourite lion, Brutus, also starred in a Caltex film about the East African Railway called *The Permanent Way*, and in an early version of the film *Maneaters of Tsavo*.

Africa's Big Five

Des Bartlett: the father of them all

In the words of Alan Root, 'Des was the Original wildlife cameraman – the archetype that so many of us youngsters learned from and tried to emulate'. There can surely be no higher praise.

Des Bartlett was born in the Queensland rainforest on 2 April 1927. His father was a teacher, who had one of the largest collections of butterflies in Australia, and was interested in everything. Des grew up to be like him – fascinated by nature. After leaving school, he got a job in a bank which he did not enjoy. A visit to the local library changed his life – he read Osa Johnson's *I Married Adventure* and became determined that he too would travel the world with a camera. He bought a camera and read all the books he could find on photography, processing, filming and editing, and left the bank to join a photographic business in Melbourne. He worked with Noel Monkman, who had made something of a name for himself as a cameraman. Armand Denis had seen Monkman's film, and offered him a job which he accepted. Des was to be his assistant, shooting the film *Wheels Across Australia*. Noel Monkman then had an accident on the barrier reef, gashing his leg badly on the coral, an injury that took a very long time to heal. So it was Des who shot the film for Armand Denis in 1952 which was the start of a very long association that changed forever the content, style and standard of wildlife filmmaking.

During the filming of *Wheels across Australia*, Des needed to buy more film stock. In those days this was obtainable from a chemist's shop, and he met Pat Edmondson whose wife worked in such a shop near Ayre's Rock. Pat later introduced Des to his sister, Jen, in Sydney.

The meeting was brief, and Des then went off to New Guinea to film *Among the Headhunters*. Jen started to excel as a tennis player, playing with Darlene Hard, Mo Connolly and the awesome 'Muscles' (Ken Rosewall). A young Fred Stolle was her ball boy. She then moved to London, and played at Wimbledon with the likes of Rod Laver. Her boat trip to London was delayed, and Des flew to Aden to meet her during her five-hour stop there.

Armand Denis was delighted with Des's footage in Australia and New Guinea, and in 1954 offered him a six-month contract to film in Africa. Des started filming in Kenya and Uganda, which resulted in six half-hour shows that were aired on the BBC. Among the first of these was *We Capture a Baby Elephant*. The baby in question was the first that David Sheldrick adopted, and his name was Samson. Daphne was at the time married to Bill Woodley, but later married David. She became involved with orphaned elephants, and never looked back. Today she is still caring for orphaned elephants in the Nairobi and Tsavo National Parks. Des just kept turning the camera, filming anything and everything that he came across. Monitor lizards and marabous in Uganda, penguins, ostriches and aardvarks in South Africa, the Victoria Falls in Rhodesia, pygmies and okapi in the Congo.

Des and Jen met up once more in 1956 and were married in London, when Jen gave up her tennis to travel to Africa with Des. Armand and Michaela were seldom with him in the field, and the programme links were filmed separately. The six-month contract turned into fourteen years, during which time Des shot 105 *On Safari* programmes (seventy of them in Africa), three colour specials, two black and white specials, and 104 shorts aired in the US under the title *Animaland*. Their daughter Julie was born in Australia in 1957. An early *On Safari* in 1956 was called *The Egg and the Snake* and involved a young schoolboy in Nairobi with a passion for snakes. His name was Alan Root, and together Des and Alan filmed an egg-eating snake swallowing a dove's egg. Des and Alan became lifelong friends, and Des was best man at Alan's wedding to Joan Thorpe in 1961.

Des and Jen filmed all over Africa, in Surinam, South America, and in the US. The last film for Armand Denis was shot in Florida in 1965, when Armand's health was failing, and Des decided to join Survival. While in Florida, they met David Hughes and persuaded him to return to South Africa and start filming, as opposed to still photography, which he was doing at the time. The Bartletts stayed in the Americas for twelve years, during which time they filmed many programmes for Survival. Travelling from the Arctic to the Antarctic, they filmed everything from bears, bison and beavers to whales, and became an Emmy award winning team, and frequent contributors to *National Geographic* magazine. Their 1973 film *Flight of the Snow Geese* is still regarded as one of the best wildlife films ever made. In 1975 they returned to Australia for two years and made a kangaroo film. In 1977 they embarked on a five-month trip on the Lindblad Explorer, recce-ing the Amazon, the West Indies, the Pacific and Indonesia. The following year they moved to Etosha where they stayed for six years, and made fourteen films.

In 1984, the Bartletts went independent, and began making films on the Skeleton Coast and in the Namib Desert. Both had learned to fly early on in their marriage, and they bought a couple of microlights which were ideal for filming in the desert. In 1995, Des had an accident in the desert, when his microlight crashed. His passenger Mary Plage was injured and Des badly damaged his ankle, always walking with a limp afterwards.

Des was one of the most meticulous people I have ever met. He had a list of birthdays and wedding anniversaries for almost everyone he knew, he logged every sequence he shot, and from his countless notebooks he calculated in 2002 that he had shot well over 2,000,000 feet of film.

Having first met Des in 1955, and again briefly at the Wildscreen festival, it was not until 2006 that I got to know him and Jen well. When Michaela Denis died in 2003, her house in Muthaiga was left empty for some time. In 2005 it was sold, and the new owner (Kenya's

President Mwai Kibaki) wanted it to be renovated. An architect friend of mine, Jim Archer, got the job, and went to inspect the property. In an outside building, he found a tangled heap of old film, about four feet high. There were only about half a dozen cans, and very little of the film was on spools. It was as if a child had been in there and unrolled every foot of film, tearing and creasing it, and then tossing it aside. Jim realised that this pile of nitrate film, which smelled as if it might self-ignite at any moment, must surely be important. He knew of course who the Denises were, and had also been at school with Alan Root. He also knew that my work involved film, so he told me of his find. I immediately phoned Alan, who agreed with me that it was essential that this film be salvaged and suggested that I got hold of Des, which I did. Des and Jen then started to make a plan to come to Nairobi and see for themselves whether this old film was worth saving. Jim Archer and I went to the house on a rescue mission. We struggled for most of a morning, trying to untangle the mass of celluloid, and eventually could do no better than scoop it up in armfuls and transfer it into Jim's vehicle – a large empty Landrover Discovery. By the time we had finished, there was film up to the roof, all over the floor, under the seats and trying to escape through the windows. We could barely close the rear door. How Jim drove back to my house, I really do not know – there was film all round the gear stick, all over the dashboard, under his feet and round the pedals, and he could see nothing in the rear view mirror but black ribbons of film. The smell was appalling, but we could not open the windows in case errant pieces escaped. But we got it back to my house, where we managed to stuff it into four or five very large packing cases, each about three feet high. It was so badly damaged already that there really was no point in trying to take care, though we did our best.

Des and Jen made their plan – they would arrive on 14 January 2006. Everyone was looking forward to their visit, and several get-togethers with old Survival people were arranged. Then tragedy struck – Joan Root was shot early in the morning of 13 January. When I went to the airport to meet Des and Jen, I wondered how I would break the news.

As soon as I saw them, I could tell that they already knew. They had bumped into Kim Wohluter in Johannesburg, and he had told them. It was so sad, they were just too late to see their old friend again.

The Bartletts stayed with me for a month. We borrowed an old gadget from Bob Campbell to wind the film on to spools, and set them up with a special table in the office. Jen wore white gloves, and had a small lens. Painstakingly they started to clean up, checking what was there. For eight to ten hours a day, they worked. At weekends they played – a short trip to the Maasai Mara with Bob and Alan, a lunch with Musa Quraishy who used to process their film, and in between film crews I did my best to make them feel at home. In the evenings we talked and found that we had many friends in common. They were the easiest guests, a real pleasure to have around and I felt incredibly honoured. One evening, at around 5 o'clock, my old tortoise Sid started digging in the rose bed. I called Des and Jen immediately. Des said 'unless I'm very much mistaken, I'd say she is about to start laying some eggs for you'. And she did. I had always been under the impression that Sid was a male, though I was wrong. However, Charles Darwin made the same mistake with a Galapagos tortoise he named Harry until one day she had to be re-named Harriet, so I did not feel so bad. Des had filmed marine turtles laying, but never a leopard tortoise. I got my little video camera, and recorded the entire operation. Darkness came, and Jen immediately stepped in as lighting expert. The old girl laid sixteen eggs, but sadly they never hatched.

We kept in touch on a regular basis, exchanging emails. Des and I talked about our respective books, and streams of questions went both ways. It was with sadness that I received an email from Jen early in July 2009 saying that Des had had a stroke. Despite the best medical care, he passed away on 12 September 2009.

Des was a pioneer. The new medium of television in the early 1950s started a whole new ballgame. While the young David Attenborough and Charles Lagus were starting out in Sierra Leone for the first *Zoo Quest* in 1954, Des was already filming in Kenya for Armand Denis.

Bob Campbell

Bob Campbell was born in Harrow, England, on 29 October 1930. His parents had come to Kenya in 1924, but his mother chose to return to England for Bob's arrival into the world. The infant Bob and his mother returned to Kenya in 1930, to the family farm in Kitale, west of the Great Rift Valley. Bob attended primary school in Kitale before moving to the Prince of Wales School in Nairobi. After the end of the Second World War, he moved to England, where he attended Cranleigh School in Surrey. He returned to Kenya at the end of 1948, and bought his first camera, an Ensign. He got a job as foreman for the township of Kitale, and then joined the Kenya Agricultural Experimental Station as a field assistant before being transferred to the Plant Breeding Station at Njoro. He then moved to Nairobi, working for E.A. Oxygen who paid him enough to purchase another camera, a Kodak Retina 35mm. In 1953 when the country was in a 'state of emergency', he joined the Kenya Regiment (as all young men had to do), and went for six months' military training in Salisbury, Rhodesia. On returning to Kenya he was transferred to the Kings African Rifles, A Company, 23rd Battalion. After being demobbed in 1955, he returned to E.A. Oxygen and bought a Jaguar XK120. He liked this car so much that he became quite an expert, and then joined the Jaguar agents in Nairobi as a mechanic. The company went under in 1956, and Bob with two friends took on the Jaguar franchise themselves.

In 1959, Bob met his wife Heather, a vet, and they married in 1961. Through Heather, Bob met Des Bartlett who was at the time filming for Armand Denis, and some of his captive animals required veterinary attention from time to time. Des lent Bob a Linhof camera, among others, and taught him how to process film, in Des's dark room. Bob then graduated to a Hasselblad and became more serious about stills photography. He established the Jaguar agency as a running concern, and gained a lot of dark room and processing experience at the same time. In 1962, Des went to film the Kariba dam operation (known as Operation Noah) where huge numbers of animals had to be rescued from the rising waters, and sent large amounts of film back to Bob for processing. Bob did such a good job that he was then offered a full time job processing film for Armand Denis Productions, as well as creating a stills library. Des took the Campbells on safari in 1963 to Amboseli, Lake Turkana (then known as Lake Rudolf), and to Murchison Falls in Uganda, to build up the stills library, and some of Bob's stills were published in *Animals* magazine.

In 1964, Des went off to America, and Bob started life as a freelance cameraman. He was invited to film one of Richard Leakey's early palaeontological expeditions to Tanzania for National Geographic. Here he learned filming the hard way with an Arri S and an odd assortment of lenses. Bob describes it modestly as 'trial and error – lots of error'. He continued to work with the Leakeys, filming for National Geographic, and then in 1965 joined two of their foreign correspondents (Frank and Helen Schreider) on a major safari in the Rift Valley. He filmed this epic 7,000 mile journey through seven countries. This association with National Geographic and Richard Leakey led to Bob joining an ABC team filming a four-hour special of *Africa*, where he ended up as a kind of roving wildlife cameraman. In between, he continued his association with Richard, documenting the excavation of fossils all over east Africa.

In 1966, Des returned briefly from America, and started to wind down Armand Denis Productions. Bob became an independent producer, and finished off the ABC project. While in the Serengeti, he met George Schaller, and contributed to his work by noting the movements of George's tagged lions. The *Africa* show aired in 1967 to great acclaim, and won an Emmy. In 1967, another long expedition took Bob to the Omo River. Then there was an assignment with Lee and Marty Talbot, where Bob filmed his first cheetah kill, before going to the western side of Lake Turkana to shoot a National Geographic lecture film for Louis and Richard Leakey. This was followed by another Leakey trip on the eastern side of the lake.

After four years, it was beginning to look as if Bob had become a permanent cameraman for the Leakeys, but in 1968 this changed suddenly and unexpectedly, and a new chapter began. Alan Root was bitten by a puff adder. This was extremely serious, and Alan nearly lost his life. He was to have gone to Rwanda, but was unable to do so. This situation brought a new direction for Bob, who was asked by Louis Leakey to go in place of Alan and take care of Dian Fossey's camp in the Virungas, and film some gorillas while Dian was away in America. He spent some eight weeks there on his own, with an Arri 16S, filming gorillas until Dian returned. Bob then returned home, and almost immediately went off to Manyara, in Tanzania, to film an elephant being darted and collared by a young Iain Douglas Hamilton. The trip was made memorable by a dominant female named Boadicea, who charged and impaled Bob's Landrover with her tusks. National Geographic subsequently asked Bob to return to Rwanda and get more gorilla footage. He flew to the US for a briefing on Dian's research work, and then went back to Rwanda, this time with a Beaulieu camera. He stayed there, with only very brief breaks, for three and a half years.

This period of his life has been amply covered in books and films, and without question the most accurate account is in Bob's own book, *The Taming of the Gorillas*. The Virungas cannot be described as an easy place in which to live, and Dian was not an easy person to work with. What is undeniable is that it was Bob who steered Dian's research in the right direction. She was initially very insistent that she would only 'observe from a distance', and was totally against trying to get close to the gorillas to gain their acceptance. Not a lot was known about gorillas at that time, and she was not a trained scientist, so she was very cautious that any intrusive approach on her part might change the animals' natural behaviour. She bluntly told Bob 'I don't want screwed up gorillas'. From a cameraman's point of view, this resulted in all the shots being taken with very long lenses, and Bob wanted more intimate, close up shots. It was Bob's patience and observational skills that enabled him to approach the gorillas much more closely, to the point that they accepted his presence. When Dian finally accepted that he was right, her research took on a whole new meaning and she became much more able to study the animals properly, as Jane Goodall had done with chimpanzees before her. In early 1972, he returned to Kenya to help the Leakeys entertain Prince Philip, Duke of Edinburgh, at Lake Turkana. It was here that Bob first met Aubrey Buxton, founder of Survival. They discussed future filming possibilities, and Bob ordered an Éclair camera and a Nagra sound recorder. Later that year, Bob returned to Rwanda to get more footage of the habituated Group 4, and the charismatic Digit, Dian's favourite gorilla.

Dian finally threw him off the mountain, and Bob returned to Kenya and normality, going to Lake Turkana for a long assignment with Richard Leakey, during which they discovered the famous '1470' and other hominid skulls. In 1973, Bob went to the US, talked to ABC about possible work, and spent time at National Geographic working on a gorilla lecture film for Dian Fossey. On his way back, he met Aubrey Buxton and Colin Willock in London, and started more detailed discussions about possible film projects for Survival. On his return, he was soon back in Turkana with Richard Leakey and filmed the 520 mile Omo River Run from the Abalte Bridge to Kalam (Ethiopia). At the end of 1973, Bob signed up as a permanent cameraman for Survival and started work on surveying the Omo Delta and other areas around Lake Turkana, with John Heminway. He had been told by Survival 'if you get the opportunity to film wildlife, just film as much as you can, you are in the right place'. The result was Bob's first half-hour programme for Survival, *There are Warthogs at the Bottom of my Garden*. 1974 saw Bob and John Heminway starting to film at Turkana (for *The Bones of Contention*), before Bob went to Lamu to film with Lorenzo and Mirella Ricciardi (*The Voyage of the Mir-El-lah*). Second camera on *The Bones of Contention* was Martin Bell, who later joined Alan Root. After completing the filming at Lamu, Bob went to Tanzania with Dieter Plage to film ground shots of Alan and Joan Root's *Safari by Balloon*. There followed a number of half hours for Survival (*Messengers of the Gods*, *Dusts of Kilimanjaro*, *The Mysterious*

Plague and *The Land of the Maasai*, and some controlled cichlid sequences for *The Parenthood Game*), before Bob went to Zambia to assist Cindy Buxton in the Luangwa Valley (*The Last Kingdom of the Elephants*).

In 1977, Survival cameraman John Pearson was tragically killed in the Ngorongoro crater in Tanzania, whilst working on the film *Hunters of the Plains*. Bob was called in to complete the cheetah sequences for this film. Having done that, Bob moved to the Maasai Mara with Jonathan Scott, to work on his own cheetah film, *The Fastest Thing on Four Legs*, before going to the coast to film the transformed cement quarry (*How Green was my Quarry*) at Bamburi with Rene Haller. The end of the 1970s saw Bob photographing the Laetoli footprints at Olduvai for National Geographic, and making a film about baboons (*Shirley Strum and the Pumphouse Gang*), as well as *The Tallest Story*, about giraffes. In 1979, Aubrey Buxton and his daughter Cindy visited Kenya, and talked about a possible flamingo film.

In 1981, Bob and Heather took some well earned time off, travelled to Namibia to visit Des and Jen Bartlett and went to Etosha with them. They came back refreshed, and Bob started on *The Way of the Jackal* and a buffalo film (*The Big Boss*). Then followed the flamingo film (*Birds of the Burning Soda*), a hyena film (*No Laughing Matter*), and an antelope film (*The Graceful Art of Success*), followed by *The Mystery of the Flying Worms* on army worms. In 1986, he produced *The Birds from Hades* about vultures, and went back to Shirley's baboons with a film called *Moving Day for the Pumphouse Gang*. While all these films for Survival were simple, one-species programmes, it must be remembered that Bob was working alone, without the support of a team of helpers in the field. This approach worked for Bob, and it worked for Survival.

Mountain gorillas would not go away. After Dian Fossey's murder in 1985 and the release of her book *Gorillas in the Mist* in 1986, Hollywood came knocking. Warner Brothers and Universal started on the feature film in 1987, and wanted Bob to be there – they wanted him for his knowledge of the area and his intimate knowledge of the gorillas more than to verify the accuracy of the story, but his official position was stills photographer. He found it very strange, seeing a story with which he had been so closely involved being changed and dramatized for the big screen. Seeing himself being played by Australian actor Brian Brown must have been an extraordinary experience. Two more different people you could not expect to meet – Brian a brash Australian and Bob a quiet, modest Brit. Second unit cameraman was Simon Trevor. In 1988, the final filming for *Gorillas in the Mist* was done at Shepperton Studios, and Bob started thinking about writing a book on his own experiences in Rwanda. He had not been able to do this before as Dian had forbidden him to put anything in print until her own book was published. Bob attended the premières of the film in New York and Los Angeles, finally left Survival in 1990, and then began to start writing in earnest. His book *The Taming of the Gorillas* was released at the London Book Fair in 2000. Since then, Bob has eased into retirement, marketing stills and doing very occasional filming.

The first time I needed Bob's help was for a film called *A Tale of Two Crowns* in 1993, produced by Richard Brock. Our resident raptor expert, Simon Thomsett, had been observing a Crowned Eagle nest in the Karen forest, on the outskirts of Nairobi. He noticed that the female had something wrong with one eye, and thought this might be something that could be repaired. Simon ascended the tree and caught the bird – no mean feat, as Crowned Eagles are known for catching monkeys (and even small children). The largest of our eagles, the Crowned, is a seriously impressive bird. Cameraman John Aitchison was doing the filming for Richard, and we all ended up in the Kikuyu Eye Hospital where the legendary (human) eye surgeon Mark Wood was waiting along with vet John Richardson. The bird, held by Simon, was then examined using the hospital's autorefractor. Her retina was damaged, and the two experts did not think it could be saved. There was an alarming moment when Simon suddenly went white, and clasping the bird to his chest gasped 'her heart has stopped'. Somehow he revived her, and all was well. Then Simon kept the bird under observation for some time, and Richard and John left the country. When the time came to release the bird back into her forest, we needed someone to film the release – Bob kindly got his old Éclair camera out of storage and filmed this sequence for us.

Later that same year, we had a crew from New York making a film about the Wildlife Crisis Campaign. They wanted to interview the then head of Kenya Wildlife Service, David (Jonah) Western, but had no cameraman and no sound recordist. Once more I called on Bob. Again he pulled his faithful camera out of storage, along with the Nagra sound recording machine that he had bought when he was in Rwanda more than twenty years earlier. He gave me a crash course on how to operate the Nagra, charged up his aged and failing camera batteries, and we went and filmed the interview at the Westerns' house on the edge of the Nairobi National Park. The house is on the edge of a cliff, and the interview was filmed outside. Bob's position on a steep slope was somewhat precarious.

Bob is a quiet and modest man, who does not consider himself to have been a 'great' cameraman. For me, his place as one of my big five is well deserved.

Hugo van Lawick

Hugo was born in Indonesia on 10 April 1937. His father was a pilot, who was killed in the war when Hugo was very small. His mother took Hugo briefly to Australia, and then to England where he attended a school in Devon. When he was ten, they moved to The Netherlands where Hugo attended school and then joined up for a year and a half of national service.

From the age of about fifteen, Hugo wanted to work with animals, and as soon as he could afford it, he bought a Bolex camera. He met Armand and Michaela Denis in Amsterdam, and travelled to Kenya to join them in 1959. He became a good stills photographer, and also learned filming with Des Bartlett at Baringo and Bogoria. During the 'learning process', Des sent Hugo off to film some tent spiders in a tree. A branch broke, and Hugo ended up falling into a river, breaking his leg and hurting his back. The nurses at the hospital asked what he had been doing to break his leg, and Hugo explained that he had been filming caterpillars. The nurses roared with laughter, and asked 'do caterpillars really run that fast?' He filmed a rhino capture in the Nairobi National Park in 1962, and then left Armand Denis to join the Game Department to catch more rhinos. During his time in Nairobi, he stayed with Louis and Mary Leakey, and made a lecture film for Louis and National Geographic. He was present at Olduvai to film the discovery of *Homo Habilis*, and also Richard Leakey's discovery of the *Zinjanthropus* jaw at Lake Natron. Hugo was invited to Washington, and signed on to work for National Geographic for five years.

One of Hugo's first assignments was a lecture film for Jane Goodall, which was followed by a television programme in 1960 called *My Friends, the Wild Chimpanzees,* which was accompanied by a book of the same name. His six-week trip to Gombe stretched to three months, and he filmed chimpanzees eating meat and using tools. Established scientists denied that chimpanzees ate meat, or used stems of grass to catch termites, and questioned Jane's work. But Hugo's footage proved her right and he set out to obtain more. He returned to Gombe for several months, then for several months more, and finally moved to Tanzania to spend six months a year at Gombe and six months a year in the Serengeti. He and Jane were married, and their son Grub was born on 4 March 1967. National Geographic released *Jane Goodall and the Wild Chimpanzees* in 1963, and Hugo continued to film the chimpanzees of Gombe. Eventually all this footage was put together into the ninety-minute film *People of the Forest*, released in 1988. The film won two Emmys and a Peabody award.

Hugo wanted to make a film on wild dogs, and while in the Serengeti he did just this, resulting in the film *The Wild Dogs of Africa* in 1974, which won another two Emmys. He released a book in 1971 called

Innocent Killers and another in 1973 called *Solo, the Story of an African Wild Dog*. Another film released in 1974 in the BBC's *World About Us* series was *The Baboons of Gombe*, which received two more Emmys. Throughout the 1970s and 1980s, Hugo continued to make films for television, and rented an edit room from Partridge Films in London to work on *People of the Forest*. This began a long association with Mike Rosenberg of Partridge Films. Mike was keen for young, up-and-coming filmmakers to get experience in Africa, and arranged for a steady stream of them to spend time at Hugo's camp at Ndutu, in the Serengeti. Many of today's leading filmmakers got into the industry through this route: Patrick Morris, Sophie Buck, Gil Dom, Matt Aeberhard, Linda Bell, Jim and Teresa Clare, Marguerite Smits van Oyen, Dave Houghton, Gus Christie, Karen Hoy to name but a few. This band of youngsters, known affectionately as 'Hugo's babies' had the best possible training. Hugo watched over them all, helping them to learn about animal behaviour, camera work, sound recording, editing, and all about making films in the greatest wildlife set on earth: the Serengeti.

Hugo kept on with his stills photography, and published several more books over the years, including *Savage Paradise* in 1977, *Sand River* with Peter Mathiessen in 1981, *Last Days in Eden* with Elspeth Huxley in 1984, *Among Predators and Prey* in 1986, and *Wild Dogs of Africa* in 1993.

Hugo really wanted to make films for the big screen, although *People of the Forest* had not been a great box office success. In 1995, Tim Cowling of Discovery asked Hugo to make a 35mm film for theatrical release. This became *The Leopard Son*. While beautifully shot, the film did not do very well except in the Netherlands, possibly due to the somewhat soporific narration by the late actor Sir John Gielgud. Following this, Hugo embarked on a partnership with Nature Conservation Films in the Netherlands. He had received the Order of the Golden Ark from Prince Bernhard of the Netherlands in 1992, and as a Dutch baron was regarded with huge esteem in that country. NCF made more than thirty films out of Ndutu, of which Hugo was executive producer for fifteen. Many of these used 'Hugo's babies'. Matt Aeberhard filmed *The Monkey Hunters*, *Playing in Savage Paradise*, *The Golden Dog*, and *The Waiting Game*. Sophie Buck filmed *The African King*, *The Lioness's Tale*, and *The Lion's Share*. Patrick Morris and Alastair McEwen came up with *Africa's Paradise of Thorns*. Hugo also started work on another full length, big screen feature entitled *Serengeti Symphony*, with Matt Aeberhard as second camera. This film has very little narration, and the sound track for the most part is classical music. The wildlife footage is spectacular, and it is a shame that the film, again, did not do very well at the box office.

Hugo's health began to fail, and he suffered from emphysema. As a long-time smoker, this was perhaps inevitable. Towards the end of his life he had to have oxygen close at hand all the time, and when he attended the Wildscreen festival in 2000 he was in a wheelchair. He received a Panda that year for outstanding achievement, but was less excited about that than about the fact that about forty of his 'babies' had gathered in Bristol for a very happy reunion. At the awards ceremony, the entire audience rose to give Hugo a standing ovation (with the exception of two very well known 'legends' in the business who firmly remained seated in what might be considered to have been the height of bad manners).

Hugo was given honorary citizenship of Tanzania in recognition of his films. He donated his footage to the government for them to use in promoting the Serengeti. Hugo died on 2 June, 2002. In his own way, he was a legend in his own right, and a true gentleman.

Simon Trevor

Simon Trevor, son of a civil engineer, was born in Surrey, England, on 25 August 1938. The family moved to Northern Rhodesia (now Zambia) in 1945 and Simon attended school at Bulawayo in Zimbabwe and Michaelhouse in South Africa. His father gave him a camera when he was fourteen, as a reward for building a water tank on their farm.

At the age of seventeen he was hired as an apprentice engineer on the Kariba dam, monitoring water levels. At nineteen he decided he did not want to become an engineer, so bought a Landrover and headed north, to Kenya. He got to know the country and its wildlife by guiding safaris for the Overland Company and in 1959 became a game warden, working in Tsavo, Amboseli and Nairobi. He bought his first Arriflex for £450 when there were only four in the country, and lent this to Alan Root for a film on poaching for the *Reader's Digest*. Bad hearing prevented him from making a career in national parks, as a necessary part of the job required firing a rifle, which did his hearing no good at all. He then decided to take up filmmaking full time.

In 1962 he joined Armand Denis and Des Bartlett, filming *Operation Noah* at Kariba dam. Des suggested to Simon that it would be a good idea to learn how to edit his own footage, as that was the best way of acquiring good camera techniques. Simon stayed with Armand Denis for nearly two years, learning from and working with Des in Botswana and the Congo. This footage was never aired as Armand's contract with the BBC was not renewed. However he did complete a half-hour film called *The Lioness*, which received the highest ratings ever for *On Safari*. He then went independent, and worked as third unit cameraman on a feature called *The Last Safari* directed by Henry Hathaway and starring Stewart Grainger. Part of this was filmed in Tsavo, and Simon, like Armand Denis and Al Milotte before him, used a 'coffin' to film hippos underwater at Mzima. In 1964 he worked with producer Ivan Tors, filming *Cowboy in Africa* with director Andrew Marton (who directed the chariot race in *Ben Hur*). Ivan Tors released some of this footage as a separate film in the US entitled *Elephant Country* in 1971. Ivan Tors was also connected with ABC, and Simon was seconded to film some programmes for the *American Sportsman* series, notably one with Bing Crosby and Phil Harris, and another with Texan governor John Connolly.

In 1964–5 Simon worked briefly for the Ker & Downey Safaris, filming safaris for clients, and also filmed shoebill storks in Uganda for the BBC. In 1967, he filmed a television series, *Africa, Texas Style*, which was a spin off from *Cowboy in Africa*. He then moved to Tsavo National Park, and was director of photography for Bill Travers on a film featuring one of Daphne Sheldrick's orphaned elephants (*An Elephant called Slowly*). From there he moved on to another feature, *Adventure in Africa* with George Plimpton.

Following this, Simon started working in earnest on a full-length feature, *The African Elephant*. He directed and photographed this over a period of time, and spent eight months in Hollywood when it was being edited. This film was nominated for an Oscar for photography, also a Golden Globe, and won the Hollywood Press Association award for the 'best English language foreign film'. It was released in ten languages, sometimes under the title *King Elephant*.

In the early 1970s, Simon joined up with Bill Travers again and filmed some sequences of *The Lion at World's End* (1971), and all of *Christian the Lion* (1972).

In 1974 Simon was second unit on a feature called *Visit to a Chief's Son*, produced by Robert Halmi, and in 1975 made a film called *The Ivory Poachers* for the Wildlife Clubs of Kenya, which was narrated by Kenya's then Attorney General, Charles Njonjo. This was followed by a film for the World Wildlife Fund (WWF), *Africa, forest or desert?* funded by the sale of a painting by David Shepherd. During the filming, Simon went to Rwanda and met up with Dian Fossey who called him 'a leech, sucking the blood of her gorillas'.

In 1976, Simon revisited the ABC *American Sportsman* programme, with a film on poaching in Tsavo, narrated by John Huston. Huston was at the time shooting *The Man Who Would Be King* in Morocco with Sean Connery and Michael Caine, and recorded the narration for Simon's film in his bedroom.

In 1978, David Attenborough and Richard Brock from the BBC visited Simon in Tsavo and looked at some of his footage. They were particularly interested in a sequence of a lung fish, and indicated that they would like Simon to shoot this again for the series *Life on Earth*. They never came back to him. Shortly after the BBC's visit, Colin

Willock from Survival also visited Simon, as Alan Root had suggested that he should look at Simon's footage. Willock offered Simon a contract to make films for Survival, but Simon refused because he would not be allowed in the editing room.

Simon then formed a collaboration with Bill Travers, to complete two films, *Bloody Ivory* and *River of Sand*. With Travers's help, both the BBC and Survival rates were increased to an acceptable level, and *Bloody Ivory* was aired in the BBC's *World About Us* series in 1978. *Bloody Ivory* was nominated for a BAFTA, and won the 'best of festival' at the Audubon International Environmental Film Festival. *River of Sand* was shown on Survival, and was then followed by several more films: *The Walking Birds, Two of a Gang* and *The Meanest Animal in the World* in 1984, *Birds of a Feather* in 1985, and *Together they Stand* in 1986, which won the Golden Panda at Wildscreen in 1986. More films for Survival were *Tumbler in the Sky* and *The Rains Came*. In this last film a dry line in the commentary was Simon's way of voicing his disappointment that the BBC never got back to him for his lung fish sequence: 'the lung fish is one of the earliest relics of life on earth'. I wonder if David and Richard ever realised this.

In 1981, Simon was co-director and director of photography for a Japanese feature called *A Tale of Africa*. It was also marketed as *Green Horizons* and *Afurika Monogatari*, and starred James Stewart. The next year, Simon shot a French feature called *In the Footsteps of the Elephants*, directed by Philippe de Brocca.

In 1985 Simon was asked by Steven Spielberg to shoot an African sequence for *The Colour Purple*. This involved giraffes running across the plains with a sunset in the background and a girl dancing in the foreground. The storyboard he was given did not quite work, but Simon managed to get the shot and Spielberg was impressed.

Next, Simon became second unit director for the big feature film in 1985, *Out of Africa*, starring Robert Redford and Meryl Streep. Then there was another Survival special, *Daphne Sheldrick and the orphans of Tsavo*. As a wildlife cameraman capable of shooting on 35mm, he was in demand for major feature films, and he also contributed as second unit director on *Gorillas in the Mist* in 1988 and *White Hunter, Black Heart* directed by and starring Clint Eastwood in 1990. More films for Survival followed in the 1990s, including *The Tombs below Aruba* about dung beetles, *Keepers of the Kingdom* about elephants, *The Hole Story* about the life of various creatures in a tree, and *Elephants of Tsavo, Love and Betrayal*. In 1996 he worked with Robin Brown to make *The African Love Story*, starring actor Hume Cronyn whom Simon had met early in his career. This BBC film included original footage from Hume and his wife Jessica Tandy's first visit to Kenya, and looking back on that retrospectively, comparing things with the reality of a changed environment.

In 1998, Simon formed the African Environmental Filmmakers' Foundation, whose aim is to make and distribute environmental films to the local people in Kenya and Tanzania. In the ten years that the foundation has been in existence, much of Simon's old footage has been re-edited and scripted (in Kiswahili, Kikuyu, Maa, Kamba, and other African languages) and new films have been made including a film about one of Tanzania's great rivers, *The Great Ruaha River* (there is also a version of this film called *Hell or High Water, Drought of the Century*), which contains rare footage of estivating crocodiles.

There is now a selection of more than a dozen relevant films freely available for distribution including *Elephants of Tsavo, Keepers of the Kingdom, A Keeper's Diary, Running Dry, Wanted Dead or Alive, Natural Security, Black Rhino – on the Brink, Tombs below Aruba, Walking Birds, Together they Stand* and *The Meanest Animal in the World*. These films have been watched by several million Kenyan and Tanzanian youngsters, and screenings are always popular. Simon is working on a new series, *Inspiration*, focusing on individuals or small organisations in the region who are doing positive and beneficial work in the environmental field. His daughter Tanya and her husband Ian Saunders run the foundation, and they are building a production base in their beloved Tsavo to develop it further.

Alan Root

'Far too much of civilized mankind today is alienated from nature. Most people seldom encounter anything but lifeless, manmade things in their daily lives and have lost the capacity to understand living things or to interact with them. That loss helps explain why mankind as a whole exhibits such vandalism toward the living world of nature that surrounds us and makes our way of life possible.' – Konrad Lorenz

David Attenborough once described Alan Root as the most innovative cameraman the world has ever seen. Alan was born in London on 12 May 1937, and his parents moved to Kenya ten years later where Alan immediately began to show an interest in the world of nature. While at the Prince of Wales School in Nairobi, he collected snakes and filmed them with an 8mm camera. During the holidays he spent time with Myles North, who was the first known person to record African bird song. He also found and successfully reared a baby bongo, the first known person to do so, and escorted it to the Cleveland Zoo.

In 1956, Alan met Armand Denis and Des Bartlett, and together they filmed an egg eating snake at Alan's school, eating a dove's egg. Alan showed his own snake film to Armand Denis, who told Alan that he thought he should consider filmmaking as a career. Alan then borrowed a 16mm Bolex camera, and made a film on jacanas. At the age of nineteen, he won his first awards, two gold medals at the Kodak World Fair. He then briefly joined John Pearson, an East African Airways pilot, before joining Armand Denis and Des Bartlett, filming in the Serengeti. At the same time he set up a safari company with his friend Richard Leakey, and came across Bernard and Michael Grzimek who were making a 35mm film for cinema in Tanzania. The warden Myles Turner recommended Alan as a cameraman, after Michael was killed in a plane crash in the Ngorongoro crater in 1959. Alan completed the film in a year, and it became *Serengeti Shall Not Die*, winning an Oscar for 'best documentary'.

In 1960 Alan joined Ian Parker and Alistair Graham to form Wildlife Services Ltd, the first private organisation to undertake wildlife research, and started filming the effects of Kenya's serious drought. This filming continued over twenty years, eventually to become *A Season in the Sun* for Survival. In 1961, Alan and his new wife Joan joined Anthony Smith, a balloonist, on a balloon flight from Zanzibar to the Serengeti which provided four half-hour programmes for the BBC called *Balloon from Zanzibar*. After this epic project, Alan and Joan returned to film once more for Bernard Grzimek, this time for a series entitled *A Place for Animals*. This project took them to Rwanda to where they filmed mountain gorillas and introduced Dian Fossey to her first gorilla.

In 1962, Alan became the first full time cameraman for Anglia Television's new wildlife series, *Survival* and made a film in Uganda on the Karamojong people. He and Joan went to Magadi in southern Kenya to film flamingoes nesting, where they found a pitiful situation. The salinity of the lake was high, and the birds, particularly the young ones, had heavy anklets of concentrated soda which restricted their movements and made them unable to fly. A call for help resulted in many volunteers pouring into Magadi to help. The team caught the birds and removed the anklets, freeing many hundreds of birds.

The next five years saw Alan and Joan filming constantly for Survival and for Grzimek's series, all over East Africa, Australia, New Guinea, South America and on the Galapagos, producing a stream of half-hour shows, and two one hour specials. These included *The new Ark*, *The Pearl in the Desert*, *Bolt from the Blue*, *Box Me a Bongo*, *Pity the Poor Crocodile*, *Leopards and Cheetahs*, *Give a Dog a Name*, *Hell's Gate*, *A Price on Their Heads* and *Nothing Going On* and *Enchanted Isles* for Survival. For Grzimek, there was *Serengeti Has Not Died*, *Salute to the Serengeti* and *The Elephant that Walked on Air*. The Galapagos film *Enchanted Isles* was presented by Prince Philip, and given a Royal première at the Festival Hall in London where Alan and Joan were presented to Her Majesty the Queen. The film was the first British wildlife special to be aired on American television, and won a Golden Nymph at the Cannes Film Festival as well as an Oscar nomination.

In 1967, Alan went freelance and to finance his filming caught and bred bongos. These went to American zoos, and formed the basis of a breeding programme that many years later resulted in some of these rare spiral-horned antelope being successfully reintroduced to their former range on Mount Kenya and the Aberdares. He was supposed to go to Rwanda to film mountain gorillas for National Geographic, but was bitten by a puff adder in Meru. Having already received antivenin for snake bite, he reacted badly to another dose. He went into anaphylactic shock and nearly lost his life, but in the end only lost his index finger. But he was unable to go to Rwanda, and his place was taken by Bob Campbell. He made a short film about elephant cropping in Uganda called *Kill by Kindness*. Alan's first major film as a freelancer was for the BBC in 1968–9 and was called *Mzima, Portrait of a Spring*, which was followed by *Baobab, Portrait of a Tree*, also for the BBC two years later. *Mzima* won the Red Ribbon at the New York Film Festival, the Best Environmental Film at the Columbus Film Festival and Best in Festival at the National Association for Environmental Education. *Baobab* won 'best documentary' at the Chicago Film Festival, 'best wildlife film' and the Christopher Award at the Columbus Film Festival, the Red and Blue Ribbon at the New York Film Festival, Certificate of Excellence at the Audubon International Festival, Best Film of the year in Los Angeles, Best Science Film in Chicago, Best in Festival at the American Environmental Film Festival, and received an Honourable Mention in San Francisco. Alan made a film on the scientist George Schaller for National Geographic, called *Man of the Serengeti* in 1972.

The next film was something Alan had wanted to do for a long time, to follow the annual wildebeest migration. For two years he and Joan followed the herds, for *The Year of the Wildebeest*, the first film to tell the whole story. During filming, Alan learned to fly a hot air balloon in order to film the herds from the air – the first time a balloon had been used for this purpose (with the exception of the unsuccessful attempt by William Boyce and George Lawrence in 1909). The film won the Golden Gate award in San Francisco, the Christopher award in Columbus, the Red Ribbon in New York, Best of Festival at the first International Wildlife Film Festival in Missoula, Best of Festival at the National Educational Film Festival, Best Film at the Learning Audio Visual Arts Festival and the Conservation Film Award from the Outdoor Writers' Association of America. Then there was *Safari by Balloon* when the Roots flew at 24,000 feet over the top of Mount Kilimanjaro, Africa's highest mountain. This won the Paramount award in Oakland, the Blue Ribbon in New York, and the 'best documentary' at the International Aeronautic and Space Film Festival. At the end of this, Alan had two balloons and a pilot, so they set up Balloon Safaris Ltd, the world's first company to offer a one-hour dawn flight followed by a champagne breakfast.

In 1976, Alan and Joan returned to Mzima for some extra footage, and while in the water were both attacked by a hippo. One lashed out at Joan, breaking her face mask with its tusk (mercifully she was unharmed), before grasping Alan's leg. This resulted in Alan being out of action for three months.

Their next project involved the life in and around a termite mound, and was called *Castles of Clay*. Everyone said it was an impossible film to make, but that only increased the Roots' determination, and the resulting film blew everyone away. It was nominated for an Oscar, won a Peabody award, was Best Science film in Birmingham, Best in Festival in Columbus, Best film at the British Association for the Advancement of Science, and received a Special Jury award in San Francisco, a Blue Ribbon in New York, the Ohio State Award for environmental film, the Diploma of Honour in Tokyo, Best Film from the Animal Behaviour Society, the Cherry Kearton award from the Royal Geographic Society, and a Continuing Career Achievement award in Missoula.

Under pressure from fans, their next film was called *Two in the Bush* (marketed in America as *Lights, Action, Africa*), which showed Alan and Joan at work. This is still one of the most popular of the Roots' films, including footage from all their major films, with behind the scenes shots showing how they managed to obtain the 'impossible' shots. Alan never rated this film very highly, but the awards poured in yet again – Diploma of Honour in Tokyo, Best in Festival at Ronda in Spain, Best Film at the Audubon Festival, Red Ribbon in New York, The Christopher award in Columbus, the Golden Gate award in San Francisco, the Golden Babe award in Chicago, the Bronze Tusker in St Louis, best editing, directing and technical accomplishment in Michigan, the Ecology award at the National Educational Film Festival.

In 1981, the Roots released *Season in the Sun*, with footage of drought and floods shot over twenty years, and showing how animals cope with the contrasting conditions. Again a stream of awards resulted, including a Peabody, an Emmy, a Wildscreen Panda award, and best in festival at the Banff festival in Canada.

Next, the Roots returned to the Serengeti to make *Salute to the Serengeti* for Survival and *Kopjes, Islands in a Sea of Grass*. Focusing on the life of these dramatic granite rocks, the *Kopjes* film contains some scenes that were 'set up' and thus criticised by some purists. There is a caracal batting a dove out of the air, and a Verreaux's Eagle catching a rock hyrax. Set-up these scenes might have been, but they depict absolutely natural behaviour which would be almost impossible to come across in the wild. The film won a Panda at Wildscreen for sound and commentary, and was runner up at the Banff festival in Canada.

The final film that Alan and Joan made together before separating was *The Legend of the Lightning Bird*, about the extraordinary nesting behaviour of the Hamerkop. This film also won a Panda at Wildscreen for cinematography.

In 1986, Alan put on another hat, becoming a guru for younger filmmakers. In the Serengeti with Richard Matthews (*Queen of Beasts*), Mark Deeble and Victoria Stone (*Here be Dragons* and *Sunlight and Shadow*), Alan began to pass on his vast knowledge and to start to hand over the mantle to younger people. *Sunlight and Shadow* won Best in Festival at Jackson, and a Panda at Wildscreen, thus launching

Deeble and Stone's career. Survival also released *Solitary Confinement* which was cut from out-takes of *Baobab*.

1987 saw Alan return to Rwanda, to film some gorilla sequences for the Warner Bros feature based on Dian Fossey's book *Gorillas in the Mist*. He was bitten in the thigh by a large silverback, adding yet again to his growing collection of battle scars.

For the ten years from 1987–97, Alan filmed in Zaire (now Democratic Republic of Congo) for Survival and National Geographic. During this time he made four major films, *Heart of Brightness* about pygmies and okapi, *Rivers of Fire and Ice* about the Virunga National Park, *The Impossible Elephants* about the old elephant training school at Garamba, and *A Space in the Heart of Africa* showing rare animals that live deep in the Congo forest. It had been thought, for instance, that the Congo peacock had been extinct since the 1930s, but Alan found and filmed this magnificent bird, along with a fishing cat and other creatures that had never before been captured on film. He certainly had not lost his touch, and these films earned him two more Pandas at Wildscreen, the best animal behaviour film and a Lifetime Achievement award at Jackson. During this time he also acted as executive producer for Deeble and Stone's award-winning films *The Tides of Kirawira*, *Little Fish in Deep Water*, *Tale of the Tides* and *Mzima, Haunt of the River Horse*. Together they also released *Serengeti Jigsaw*, and Alan received a Lifetime Achievement award at Wildscreen.

In 1997, Alan paused his filmmaking so as to care for his terminally ill second wife, Jenny, and bought a helicopter which he learned to fly. Switching from a fixed-wing Cessna to a helicopter was not without problems, and he crashed two helicopters before perfecting the art. He now uses his helicopter on various conservation projects such as translocations, darting exercises, and game counts.

In recent years Alan also received a Lifetime Achievement award from the New York Environmental Film Festival, and the Filmmakers for Conservation award at the Wildscreen Festival. In 2007 he was awarded the OBE. Now remarried with two small sons, he spent two years in the Serengeti filming wildlife sequences for a Hollywood feature based on the life of Bernard Grzimek. The film is now seemingly stuck in the Hollywood pipeline.

Following the tragic murder of Alan's first wife Joan in January 2006, Alan has been consulted on two films based on her life – a documentary by Henry Singer entitled *Murder on the Lake* shown on the BBC in early 2010, and a Hollywood feature starring Julia Roberts, which again is stuck in the Hollywood pipeline. Alan has recently built a house on the Lewa Wildlife Conservancy, where he lives with his wife Fran and their two sons Myles and Rory.

Other Special People

Joan Root

'The greatness of a nation and its moral progress can be judged by the way its animals are treated.' – Mahatma Gandhi

I cannot possibly put this book to bed without including my friend Joan Root who was tragically murdered in January 2006. As everyone knows, Joan was married to Alan for more than twenty years, and he is the first to admit that he could not have achieved what he did without her. At her memorial service on the shores of Lake Naivasha, Alan described her as 'the wind beneath his wings'. She was all that, and more. A quiet and reserved person, Joan did not want anything to do with being in the limelight. She was incredibly capable, and before she met Alan she worked with her father organising safaris. This is something that many Kenya women do in their sleep, packing up the camping equipment, organising the food supplies, making sure the medical kit is fully stocked, planning everything in minute detail. With Alan she did all that automatically, never quite knowing where the next filming trip would take them or how long it would last.

In addition, she was Alan's producer, production assistant, location manager, accountant, and cook. She logged the footage, she handled the shipping of rushes, she paid the bills, she learned to fly, she drove the camera vehicle, and more. When Alan was filming she was beside him, often with a stills camera, climbing trees, scaling cliffs, fording rivers, flying a hot air balloon, diving with hippos, or making tea. She loved the life, and there was nothing that she would not do to help Alan achieve the perfection he sought.

One of the things that had attracted Alan to Joan in the first place, aside from her beauty, was her empathy with animals. When he first met her, she was raising a baby elephant. Over the years, she tended all manner of creatures, birds, reptiles and mammals. When asked how many animals she had cared for, she did not really know but thought it was probably several hundred. It has been said that she tended every species from aardvark to zorilla, and many more in between. On the first occasion when she came to stay with me in Nairobi, she had with her two very small weaver chicks that had fallen out of a nest. They had no feathers and were totally helpless. Instead of sitting Joan down with a drink and something to eat, I found myself on my hands and knees on the lawn for an hour or so, collecting insects. On subsequent visits, she came with a duiker, a house snake, or a crane. One day we found some very large caterpillars which she judged to be some kind of emperor moth, and she took some with her so that she could identify them when they hatched.

When Alan and Joan separated, it took Joan a long time to 'find herself' again. She retreated to the shores of the lake and concentrated on all the animals that lived there, learning more about the plants and the ecology of the lake itself. She became passionately involved with trying to save the lake, which was being over-fished and whose waters were being contaminated by the proliferation of agriculture on its shores, predominantly the growing of roses and carnations for export. She could see that the balance of nature was out of kilter, and did her best to make it better. Sadly, it was an almost impossible battle, and one which she could never win. She did not deserve to die in such a brutally violent way. My gentle, kind, and loving friend: rest in peace.

Top: Joan Root and a young crowned crane. *Photo Jean Hartley*

Below: Alan Root filming on Mt Lengai. *Photo Reinhard Radke*

Top: One of Brian Leith's lions – the ultimate in madness.   *Photo Jean Hartley*

Below left: Mike Herd and Bill Markham filming zebras.   *Photo Bill Markham. Below right*: Hugo van Lawick at the premier of "The Leopard Son".   *Photo Alan miller*

Top left: Jen Bartlett untangling old Armand Denis film, *photo Jean Hartley. Top right:* Alan Root, *Photo Chryssee Bradley Martin*

Below: Rudi Kovanic filming elephants. *Photo Omni Productions*

Top: Jen, Des and Julie Bartlett, taken in 2009. *Courtesy Jen Bartlett*

Below: the start of it all – Adrian Warren and Hugh Maynard filming "The Great African Bird Safari Rally", 1986. *Photo John Glen*

Top: Martin and Osa Johnson's original front door (*left*) and another door (*right*) from their house at Lake Paradise. *Photos by Mia Collis Special thanks to Monty and Hilary Ruben*

Below: Armand and Michaela Denis on set in Amboseli, 1950s. Des Bartlett on left. *Courtesy Jen Bartlett*

Top: Bob Campbell, Des Bartlett, Alan Root, 2006. *Courtesy Jen Bartlett*

Below: Simon Trevor filming scorpions with Damian Bell. *Courtesy Simon Trevor*

The Television Era

'Why should people go out and pay money to see bad films when they can stay at home and see bad television for nothing?' – Samuel Goldwyn

'If a show sucks, it still sucks even if you can see it in high-def.' – Eric Schotz, LMNO Productions

While television had been around for a number of years, the making of African wildlife films for television during the 1950s and 1960s was mostly restricted to people who lived here – Armand and Michaela Denis and my big five. David Attenborough's *Zoo Quest* in the mid-1950s had been very popular, but he himself resisted coming to East Africa. As he said, 'I realized I was on a hiding to nothing, with people like Armand Denis and Alan Root actually *living* there and being able to devote far more time than I could'. His one exception was for the film *Elsa the Lioness*, when he was persuaded to divert to Meru while passing through Kenya on his way to Madagascar in 1960.

In the late 1950s and early 1960s, Alan Root and Bernard Grzimek were producing films in Tanzania, Hugo van Lawick was in Gombe with Jane Goodall. *Elsa the Lioness* had hit the screens, Lewis Cotlow was filming *Zanzabuku*, the Milottes were working on *The African Lion* for Disney, and Carr Hartley's animals were being used increasingly by Hollywood. In the mid-1960s, Simon Trevor and Bob Campbell were working in Kenya, and the ABC *American Sportsman* series was in full swing in Kenya and Tanzania. In 1969, Alan moved back to Kenya to make his first two films for the BBC (*Mzima* and *Baobab*), but it was not until 1970 that the next BBC producer ventured to Kenya with a crew. This was Ned Kelly, whose film *African Seafari* was part of the series *The World About Us*, and was filmed at Watamu and Malindi on the Kenya coast. In the early 1970s, Jack Couffer was director of photography for the second Elsa film *Living Free* and the *Born Free* television series, and also filmed one sequence for *The Darwin*

Adventure at Lake Baringo. In 1972, a BBC producer Richard Brock arrived in Kenya to make part of a film *Around the World in 80 Minutes*, and a series for *The World About Us* called *Web of Life*. Richard had spent time in Nairobi before Kenya's independence, with the Royal Air Force doing national service, and developed an affection for the country which endures to this day.

By this time, Survival had also established a presence in Kenya, with Bob Campbell, Simon Trevor and Alan Root all living here. In 1973, Aubrey Buxton's daughter Cindy came to make her first film, *The Floating World of Lake Naivasha*. Dieter Plage ventured into Tanzania to work with Iain Douglas Hamilton on *The Family that Lives with Elephants*. Richard Brock returned again for *The World About Us*, to film part of the series *A Taste for Adventure* – notably a film on the legendary game warden Bill Woodley called *Bill's Big Hill*, followed by *What Use is Wildlife?*. George Inger made a film on the sculptor Jonathan Kenworthy, called *Kenworthy's Kenya*, and John Sparks brought Maurice Tibbles to make a zebra film called *The Day of the Zebra*. In 1977, Robin Hellier produced a controversial film about ivory poaching, using local cameraman Mohinder Dhillon. This was called *The Elephant Run*, and covered a very sensitive subject at that time in Kenya's history. The film revealed that the family of President Kenyatta was heavily involved in the illegal ivory trade. Mohinder's sound man Abdul Kayum was arrested, and Mohinder was summoned by the immigration authorities and given ten days to leave the country. It was only through intervention from hotelier and WWF member Jack Block and Attorney General Charles Njonjo that the expulsion order was lifted. The film was aired on British television on the night of the Queen's Silver Jubilee. Since most people in the UK were watching the Queen, the elephant film escaped the notice of the Kenyan High Commissioner in London.

While Bob Campbell, Cindy Buxton, and Simon Trevor produced programme after programme for Survival, Alan and his wife Joan were working on *Castles of Clay*. The BBC's Barry Paine and cameraman Hugh Maynard produced a giraffe film *Africa's Tallest Story* in Tanzania, and Adrian Warren came to Kenya to produce his first film for the BBC. Using local cameraman, Mohinder Dhillon, the film was *Last Chance for the Grevy*, for the series *Wildlife on One*.

The last year of the 1970s brought the blockbuster *Life on Earth*, several sequences of which were filmed in Kenya. Following this, in 1980, Richard Brock renewed his love affair with Kenya and made *The Impossible Bird* and *Red River Safari* with Hugh Miles, both for *Wildlife on One*. The early 1980s was again dominated by Survival (Alan, Bob, Simon and Cindy), until the next BBC blockbuster, *The Living Planet* in 1984.

1986 saw Adrian Warren from the BBC return to Kenya, and this was the first film that I worked on. *The Great African Safari Bird Rally* was a little half-hour show involving teams of competing birdwatchers. This led me on to *The Great Rift*, again with Adrian, and the formation of my company, Viewfinders. The year also marked the start of a more aggressive BBC presence in Kenya, with Keith Scholey and Hugh Miles in the Maasai Mara filming *Leopard, a Darkness in the Grass*, Alastair Fothergill filming at Soysambu (*The Bee Team* for WOO), and Marion Zunz coming for the first film about the now legendary elephant, *Echo*, in Amboseli. Before the film was completed, Marion was tragically killed in a skiing accident, and the film was completed by John Sparks. Adrian moved to Rwanda to film *Gorillas in the Midst of Man* for the BBC with cameraman Neil Rettig. We then became involved in IMAX – first for the film *Blue Planet*, which was essentially a space film with a bit of wildlife in the Ngorongoro crater and Lake Natron (both very easily visible from space). Chris Parsons had started an IMAX Natural History Unit, and this was their first project. Chris used the opportunity to conduct an IMAX camera training exercise in Tanzania, which included Neil Rettig and Richard Goss. Adrian then left the BBC and embarked on the first full-on wildlife IMAX film, about mountain gorillas in Rwanda with Neil Rettig as cameraman and Chris West on sound. Filming was curtailed by the outbreak of civil war, but everyone, including George Schaller and his wife Kaye were safely airlifted out of Rwanda by French paratroopers.

Throughout the 1990s, the number of films increased dramatically, with other companies such as National Geographic, NOVA, John Downer, Turner Broadcasting, CBC and ZDF entering the fray. Crews started coming from France, Italy, Australia and South Africa, and Viewfinders became increasingly busy. Richard Matthews struck out on his own with Zebra Films. Richard Brock had left the BBC and formed his own production company, churning out several films with the series title *Endangered*. Survival's Bob Campbell was still going strong, joined by Barbara Tyack, and more independent companies sprang up, such as Scorer Associates (Brian Leith), as well as some from the USA, including Kreatures Productions (the Kratt brothers, Martin and Chris). Discovery joined the queue, and three in their *series The Ultimate Guide to…* were filmed here. The Canadian company, Omni Productions came several times during the production of several series called *Champions of the Wild*, featuring scientists and conservationists in this part of the world. Hugo van Lawick moved into 'big screen' films with *The Leopard Son* in 1996, and we also looked after more IMAX films – *Africa's Elephant Kingdom, Africa, the Serengeti* and *Rivers of Life*. Simon King's star was rising with *Duma the Cheetah*, and a young couple called Mark Deeble and Victoria Stone were causing ripples of amazement with their beautifully crafted films.

Lions

One of my favourite producers has to be Brian Leith. He is always charming and does not get rattled. He listens, and he has made many fine films.

One of these was *The Ultimate Guide to Big Cats*, for Discovery. Much of this was filmed in the Serengeti, and Brian contacted scientist Craig Packer who has lived and worked there for many years. Craig had come up with a theory that the colour of a lion's mane was important to the females, and he used the film as an opportunity to prove this theory.

So it was one day that we received a phone call from Brian's office in Bristol, England telling us that some life-sized stuffed lions were being shipped from China, and asking the best way to get them to the Serengeti. We advised that they should be freighted to Nairobi, and we would offload them and put them on to the charter flight that was carrying the crew to Tanzania. The timing was very tight, as the crew and the lions both arrived on the same flight, and cargo is usually offloaded and cleared in a different section of the airport, far away from the passenger terminal. In this case we arranged for a 'tarmac transfer', and managed to offload the lions on the apron at the passenger terminal.

I was on the apron with the crew, and four tractors drove towards us, each pulling a huge wooden box, firmly padlocked. There was simply no way that these crates would fit into the Cessna Caravan, so we had to unpack right there, on the tarmac.

We tackled one box at a time, with a jemmy, splintering plywood and foam rubber all over the apron. One by one we loaded the stuffed lions into the Caravan, with cameraman Mike Fox filming the exercise. We lay them down on top of each other at the back of the aircraft, then loaded the crew and their equipment. Just as the pilot was getting into his seat to take off, a man came running across the tarmac with a small package in his hand, dodging all the splintered shards of wood. 'This is part of the consignment', he said, handing me the package. I opened it. Inside were four sets of keys to the padlocks. Too little, too late.

Wildlife filmmaking had reached new heights. The BBC series *Big Cat Diary* started in 1996, was repeated in 1998 and 2000 and then changed to *Big Cat Week* which was filmed annually up until 2008 when it was aired as a one-off *Big Cat Live*. This was probably the largest project we had worked on, with a crew of more than ninety people, thirty-five tons of equipment, and many logistical challenges.

Into the new century, a new breed of films began to trickle in – *Deadly African Snakes* with Steve Irwin, and several programmes featuring similar presenters. More films of this kind followed, resulting in a boom for a new type of programming. Someone somewhere had the idea that traditional wildlife films were boring, and that the way to go was to get brash, fearless, charismatic presenters to liven things up. A new breed of presenters emerged, some good and some cringingly awful. The buzz words were who will be the new David Attenborough? Nonsense indeed.

The demand for sensational reality programming seemed to be insatiable, with more channels, more production companies, more new ideas flooding the scene, all veering away from wildlife as we knew it. The trend seemed to be to produce more and more films for less and less money, inevitably lowering the standard of programming. Why spend many months, even years, making a wildlife film the hard way, showing genuine behaviour and nature at its best? Now it seemed that the producers who were in demand were those who could make a fifty-minute film in a week, and for virtually nothing. Of course, the films consist of only a tiny proportion of wildlife, and a huge proportion of time is spent with some new presenter talking to the camera, clearly with very minimal knowledge or understanding of the creatures they are talking about. All they were required to do was to be on screen, flirting with the camera, and gaining instant fame. If they could haul a terrified reptile out of its hole, or get within charging distance of a huge pachyderm, so much the better.

The problem was that a new category of film had entered the market, so that reality and entertainment genres were joined, overwhelming the wildlife programmes, with all three being lumped together by those marketing this new material. Traditional, good wildlife films at this time dipped, struggling against the competition of the brash entertainment that had overtaken the genre. To me, this two-headed monster – reality and entertainment – degraded the traditional wildlife film as we knew it. It seems that the struggle continues.

These changes had an effect on genuine wildlife filming. Survival and Partridge Films were both taken over, and subsequently disappeared. The BBC's long running series *Wildlife on One* was axed. Few production companies had enough money to make blue chip films any more; the trend was for cheap programming with very little innovation. The upper hand was no longer with the dedicated and passionate filmmakers, but rather with the commissioning editors, the business people, not the filmmakers. These people have the power to make or break a film, and there have been several years of cataclysmic breakages.

So – how did it come to this? I think the apparent thirst for the action-packed, blood stained, predatorial 'life or death' films known in some circles as 'Fang TV' goes back to the 1920s. Filmmakers such as Paul Hoefler and Martin Johnson from America came to film in Africa not because they were passionately interested in African wildlife, but out of a sense of adventure. Here was a continent filled with exotic animals (and people), which American audiences had never seen. They wanted to be the first to take back moving images of the 'dangers' of Africa, the 'excitement' of Africa, or to put it another way, to show themselves as brave adventurers, suffering untold hardships in the wild in order to bring something 'new' to the screens of America. Going right back to Theodore Roosevelt's time, not one of these camera operators had the first idea about African wildlife, and very little knowledge about wildlife of any other kind either. There were few scientists, virtually no animal behaviour experts (with the possible exception of some of the East African professional hunters who accompanied the early film makers on their travels), and no conservation organisations to advise, criticise, correct or inform. So the egos, the imaginations and the ignorance of the people who made those early films tended to win in the battle of theatrics versus truth. They apparently believed that their audiences wanted excitement. Their audiences never got anything else – and were never asked – so how could they know?

Any sensitivity and balanced attitudes towards wildlife filming were then, and still are, predominantly shown by the British filmmakers.

Nature is not filled with round-the-clock hunts, kills, battles, danger and struggles. Of course these things happen, but so too do display, courtship, birth, bringing up young, playing, caring, training, nurturing, and the whole gamut of activities that are part of the cycle of nature as a whole. Concentrating on the 'red in tooth and claw' in nature is misleading. If a film does not tell the whole story, how can it not be skewed? Where is the justification on the part of filmmakers, producers and commissioning editors for coming up with so many films that simply should not be categorised as wildlife films? If people must make 'Fang TV' shows, then at least let us not pretend that they are wildlife films, because they are not.

When I joined the industry at the end of the 1980s, the wildlife film making community (on both sides of the Atlantic) was a small and close-knit community of like-minded people. These were people with passion, both for wildlife and for filmmaking. If they had seen, or filmed something that had not been seen or filmed before, they would sit and talk about it in hushed tones, sharing the wonder of some newly discovered behaviour that had been captured on celluloid. People like Hugh Miles, Mike Richards and Hugh Maynard would watch the latest films from Martin Saunders, Dieter Plage or David Parer, and take them apart sequence by sequence. They admired and acknowledged each other's talent and respected it. Nowadays it might be Martyn Colbeck, Doug Allen and Mark Deeble watching footage by Charlie Hamilton-James, or Barrie Britton. Or it could be any of them admiring John Downer's innovative approaches in camera design. But this dedicated community has increased beyond all imagination to include another breed of people altogether. Now they are surrounded by those who want to make a one-hour film in two days, or a six-part series in a week. Their interest is not in making a beautiful, innovative, wonderfully constructed gem of a film about a particular creature, or a place, that will both entertain and educate, and create a sense of awe and wonder at the sheer beauty of the natural world. Instead their purpose seems to be to fill the screen with gash footage (often purchased from a stock library), tied together with a less than charismatic presenter who can do take after take after take at no extra expense, thrown all together with a bit of music, and handed over in exchange for a meagre cheque, before moving on to the next project. Where is the sense of pride, of achievement; where is respect for nature in this approach? Can such people honestly believe that they are wildlife filmmakers? By definition, I think not. The problem is not in the range and variety of all these very different films; it is in the fact that all such films are still categorised as wildlife films, and many of them definitely belong in another genre altogether. Call me old fashioned, but many people out there agree.

A film showing a presenter in a dangerous situation with a potentially deadly animal may appeal to some audiences, who seem to need that frisson of fear to get their adrenalin racing sufficiently to get them off the couch. But they are not watching nature behaving naturally. I find these programmes very difficult to watch, because I sense that the creature is stressed, terrified and defensive. It seems to me that these films are encouraging children and young people to follow the bad example of the presenters. If a whole generation grows up thinking it is acceptable to harass reptiles or large predators by encouraging them to attack, then there is going to be a very real shortage of conservationists in the future. I remember when Steve Irwin burst on to our screens, and an eminent Australian scientist at the Wildscreen festival said that crocodile conservation had been put back ten years as a result. This is not a healthy situation.

For as long as I can remember, there have been people trying to establish some rules, such as 'Thou shalt not harm the animal'. Way back in 1937, the Cinematograph Films (Animals) Act was passed in Britain, to prevent cruelty to animals being filmed. An organisation called Filmmakers for Conservation is currently trying to control this side of things, with such luminaries as Jeffrey Boswall, Chris Palmer and Andrew Buchanan battling to ensure that there are set standards to be followed, recognised ethics to be adhered to. They say that if captive animals are used, there should be a disclaimer telling the audience so. It is my belief that intelligent audiences are fascinated by how the films are made, they love to watch the making of films, and they like to 'meet' the people behind the scenes who are responsible for the film or programme. Opening this window on 'how it is done' to the audience creates a feeling of trust from the audience towards the filmmaker. I think this is how it should be. Some audiences are not so discerning. Recently in 2008 a taxi driver in Bristol told me he had just watched an old Disney film, and he truly believed that lemmings commit suicide by throwing themselves off a cliff. I could not convince him otherwise. Surely it is the responsibility of the filmmakers to ensure that the audience learns the truth?

The most innovative filmmakers around today, in my view, are the husband and wife team Mark Deeble and Victoria Stone. They will not be rushed, and it is not unusual for them to spend three years making a film. They learned from the master – Alan Root, and people began to notice them after *Here Be Dragons* in 1989 and *Sunlight and Shadow* in 1990. *A Little Fish in Deep Water* won the Golden Panda at Wildscreen in 1996. Since then they have progressed to win more awards including Emmys and Peabodys with their films – *Tides of Kirawira, Mzima, Haunt of the River Horse, Tale of the Tides,* and *Queen of Trees*. Their next venture will be a 3-D film.

Recent technical innovations have changed the face of nature programmes even more. The Cineflex camera, attached to a heligimbal mount on a helicopter, provides aerial footage that is breathtaking. Better still, the camera lens is so powerful that the helicopter does not have to fly low and loud over the animals, but can be high enough that they do not react to its presence at all. The BBC series *Planet Earth* and more recently *Life* used this technology, and the results are visually sensational. High Definition (HD) films are also being produced for the big screen, with Disney Nature setting up in Paris. Their first film *Crimson Wing* about flamingoes, filmed in Kenya and Tanzania, was nominated for five awards at the 2009 Jackson Hole Wildlife Film Festival – receiving more nominations than any film in the festival's history. Currently in production is a film on the big cats of the Maasai Mara directed by Keith Scholey, formerly of the BBC.

This film involves two and a half years of filming, with a budget to match. Whether the new HD technology and picture quality will draw wildlife viewers back into the cinemas remains to be seen. Hugo van Lawick's experience on the big screen, with *People of the Forest*, *Serengeti Symphony* and *The Leopard Son*, was disappointing, and the only film in recent years to have had real impact in cinemas was the excellent *March of the Penguins*.

As we escape the first decade of the twenty-first century, the industry seems buoyant enough. New projects continue to pour in, and in 2010 we have two 3-D films coming. With the announcement of a dedicated 3-D channel, perhaps this is the way some wildlife films will go. Meanwhile, television seems to be the major market, with the largest audiences, although with the ever increasing choices of downloading films from the internet, this will probably change as well. The day when people do all their viewing via computer and television sets are dumped may not be far off.

A hundred years have passed since Cherry Kearton struggled to obtain images with a heavy, noisy, cumbersome wooden camera on a static tripod. He had no vehicles, particularly no camera vehicle, no spotters, no sound recordist, no producer, no fixer, no opportunity for aerials, no radios or satellite phone, and none of the luxuries that current filmmakers enjoy. He had to develop his film daily, often in the bush, and it has hard to imagine how difficult it must have been. Times have certainly changed. The quality of pictures has improved and the number of films made is unbelievable. What concerns me is whether things are going in the right direction.

I contended from the start that there are films that should never have been made at all. As the number of these increases by the minute, what is the answer? It seems to me that the commissioners are out of touch with their audiences, and that audiences are not standing up for themselves. While it is a sad fact of life that some people will watch anything, my feeling is that audiences are generally far more intelligent than the commissioners give them credit for. Can the audience not make themselves heard? Can they not demand a better product? On the other side, can the commissioners come clean and stop pretending that they are making 'wildlife films'? If they want to make sensational, adrenalin-packed programmes, can they find a way to do this without denigrating nature and wildlife? Can we put some respect for the natural world back into the formula for a good film? Can the people who make these cheap, unnatural and inaccurate 'reality' animal programmes take on a responsibility for the planet? The natural world is threatened enough, and planet earth is all we have to stand on. We should all look after it, and this includes the filmmaking fraternity who are in a position to make a difference.

One suggestion would be for all the true wildlife fixers in the world to unite and stop handling the kind of programmes that are compromising the industry. I may be a lone voice in the wilderness, but I would like to see that wilderness preserved with much more care and attention, and I would like to see a far greater sense of awe, wonder and respect for the natural world being felt by many more people.

Bibliography

Allan, Doug (2008) 'A 25 Year BBC Retrospective', International Association of Wildlife Filmmakers, March.

Akeley, Mary L. Jobe (1931) *Carl Akeley's Africa*, London: Victor Gollancz.

Akeley, Mary L. Jobe (1940) *The Wilderness Lives Again*. New York NY: Dodd, Mead & Co.

Attenborough, Sir David (2008) 'Life as we know it', *Telegraph magazine*, 5 January.

Bach, Steven (2007) *Leni: the life and work of Leni Riefenstahl*. London: Little Brown.

Bale, Peter [Series Editor, *Wildlife on One*] (1982) *Wildlife Through the Camera*. London: BBC Books.

Barnouw, Erik (1974) *Documentary – A History of Non-Fiction Film*. Oxford: Oxford University Press.

Barsam, Richard Meran (1973) *Non-Fiction Film, a Critical History*. New York NY: EP Dutton & Co Inc.

Bartlett, Des (1966) *Growing Up with Animals*. London: Collins.

Bartlett, Jen And Des (1967) *Nature's Paradise*. London: Collins.

Beinart, William and Lottie Hughes (2007) *Environment and Empire*. Oxford: Oxford University Press.

Bienvenido, Leon (1998) *Science Popularisation through Television Documentary: a study of the work of British wildlife film maker David Attenborough*, Berlin: 5th international conference of science & technology, September.

Binks, H.K. (1959) *African Rainbow*. London: Sidgwick & Jackson.

Blackhall, Sue (2007) '100 years of animal magic', *International Express*, 4 September.

Bodry-Sanders, Penelope (1991) *Carl Akeley, Africa's Collector, Africa's Savior*. New York NY: Paragon House.

Boswall, Jeffery (ed.) (1969) *Look*. London: BBC.

Boswall, Jeffery (1982) 'The ethics of Wildlife film-making: a discussion', *BKSTS Journal*, January.

Boswall, Jeffery (1998) 'Wildlife film ethics: time for screen disclaimers?', *Image Technology*, October.

Bourke, Anthony and John Rendall (1971) *A Lion Called Christian*. London: Bantam Press.

Bouse, Derek (2000) *Wildlife Films*. Philadelphia PA: University of Pennsylvania Press.

Bouse, Derek (2007) 'Book review: Cynthia Chris, watching wildlife', *International Journal of Communications* 1.

Bright, Michael (2007) *100 Years of Wildlife*. London: BBC Books.

Brown, Monty (2004) *"RJ" Richard John Cuninghame 1871–1925 – Naturalist, Hunter, Gentleman*. London: Monty Brown (privately printed).

Brown, Monty (2008) *Arthur S Waller 1882–1952, A Memoir*. London: Monty Brown (privately printed).

Brownlow, Kevin (1979) *The War, the West, and the Wilderness*. London: Secker & Warburg.

Bull, Bartle (1992) *Safari – a Chronicle of Adventure*. New York NY: Penguin Books.

Buxton, Cindy (1980) *Survival in the Wild*. London: Collins.

Campbell, Bob (2000) *The Taming of the Gorillas*. London: Minerva Press.

Chris, Cynthia (2006) *Watching Wildlife*. Minneapolis MN: University of Minnesota Press.

Cotlow, Lewis (1957) *Zanzabuku (Dangerous Safari)* the book on which the film is based. London Robert Hale.

Cottar, Charles (1999) *Cottar, the Exception was the Rule*. Auoura CA: Trophy Room Books.

Couffer, Jack (1963) *The Song of Wild Laughter*. New York NY: Simon & Schuster.

Couffer, Jack (1972) *The Lions of Living Free*. London: Collins & Harvill Press.

Couffer, Jack (2010) *The Lion and the Giraffe, a Naturalist's Life in the Movie Business*. Duncan OK: BearManor Media.

Creamer, Jon (2007) 'The natural history of TV', *Televisual*, June.

Davies, Gail (1997) 'Networks of Nature, Stories of Natural History Film making from the BBC', PhD thesis, University College London.

De Watteville, Vivienne (1935) *Speak to the Earth*. London: Methuen & Co.

Delmont, Joseph (1925) *Wild Animals on the Films*. London: Methuen & Co Ltd.

Denis, Armand (1963) *On Safari*. London: Collins.

Denis, Armand (1964) *My Life with the Animals of Africa. The rivers & lakes*. London: Collins.

Denis, Armand (1964) *My Life with the Animals of Africa. The great plains*. London: Collins.

Denis, Michaela (1955) *Leopard in My Lap*. London: W.H. Allen.

Denis, Michaela (1959) *Ride a Rhino*. London: W.H. Allen.

Dugmore, A. Radclyffe (1900) *Camera Adventures in the African Wilds*. London: William Heinemann.

Dugmore, A. Radclyffe (1925) *The Wonderland of Big Game*. London: JW Arrowsmith.

Eastman, George (1927) *Chronicles of an African Trip*. Privately printed (in the US).

Evans, Chris (2007) 'Nature filmmaking: ready for their close up', (UK) *Independent*, 7 November.

Glasgow Media Group (1998) 'What the Audience Thinks', commissioned by Wildscreen, October.

Gray, James (2002) *Snarl for the camera.* London: Judy Piatkus.

Green, Fitzhugh (1928) *Martin Johnson, Lion Hunter.* New York NY: G. P. Putnam's Sons.

Grzimek, Bernard (1960) *Serengeti Shall not Die.* London: Hamish Hamilton.

Grzimek, Bernard (1970) *Among Animals of Africa.* London: Collins.

Haigh, Jerry (2008) *The Trouble with Lions.* Edmonton AB: University of Alberta Press.

Hall, Mordaunt (1930) 'Sounds in the Jungle, Nome in 1900', *New York Times*, 20 September.

Hawkins, Desmond (ed.) (1960) *The 2nd BBC Naturalist.* London: Adprint.

Hayes, Margaret Ann (1989) *Where the Tarmac Ends.* Okanagan Falls BC: Rima Books.

Hellen, Nicholas (1998) 'Survival programme admits using captive animals as stars', *Sunday Times*, 9 August.

Hemsing, Jan (1989) *Ker & Downey Safaris, the Inside Story.* Nairobi: Sealpoint Publicity.

Herne, Brian (1999) *White Hunters.* New York NY: Henry Holt & Company.

Hoefler, Paul L. (1931) *Africa Speaks.* Philadelphia PA: John C. Winston Company.

Holt, Christopher, (1958) 'Mermaids ahoy', in *African Life*, November.

Imperato, Pascal J. and Eleanor M. (1992) *They Married Adventure.* New Jersey NJ: Rutgers University Press.

Johnson, Martin (1929) *Lion- African Adventure with the King of the Beasts.* New York NY: G.P. Putnam's Sons.

Johnson, Martin (1935) *Over African Jungles*. New York NY: Harcourt Brace & Co.

Johnson, Osa (1940) *I Married Adventure*. London: Hutchinson & Co.

Johnson, Osa (1941) *Four Years in Paradise*. New York NY: J B Lippincott Company.

Kearton, Cherry (1930) *In the Land of the Lion*. New York NY: Robert M McBride & Co.

Kearton, Cherry (1941) *Cherry Kearton's Travels*. London Robert Hale Ltd.

Kilborn, Richard (2006) 'A walk on the wild side: the changing face of TV wildlife documentary', *Jump Cut* 48, winter.

Koch, Ludwig (1955) *Memoirs of a Bird Man*. London: Phoenix House.

Leslie Melville, Betty (2000) *The Giraffe Lady*. Baltimore MD: Upland Publishing.

Madslien, Jorn (2004) 'Making wildlife films sexy', BBC News Online, 24 October.

Mitman, Gregg (1999) *Reel Nature – America's Romance with Wildlife on Film*. Cambridge MA: Harvard College.

Paice, Edward (1999) 'History: the history of safari', *Travel Africa Magazine*, Issue 10, winter.

Palmer, Chris (2007) 'Do no harm', *Realscreen* September/October, p.76.

Palmer, Chris (2008) 'About Conservation Filmmaking', *Filmmakers for Conservation*, 2 September.

Parsons, Christopher (1982) *True to Nature*. Cambridge: Patrick Stephens Ltd.

Percival, A Blayney (1924) *A Game Ranger's Notebook*. London: Nisbet & Co.

Pike, Oliver (1946) *Nature and My Cine Camera*. London: Focal Press.

Plage, Dieter (1980) *Wild Horizons, a Cameraman in Africa*. London: Collins.

Plimpton, George (1999) 'The man who was eaten alive - Alan Root's wild kingdom', *The New Yorker*, 23/30 August.

Roosevelt, Theodore (1910) *African Game Trails*. New York NY: Scribner.

Ryan, Rob and Judy (2000) *Marula*. Privately printed (in Atherton, Australia).

Scholey, Keith (ed.) (1997) *Wildlife Specials*. London: Trident Press.

Scott, Peter (1983) *Travel Diaries of a Naturalist*. London: Collins.

Scott, Philippa (2002) *So Many Sunlit Hours*. London: Wildfowl and Wetlands Trust.

Smith, Anthony (1963) *Throw Out Two Hands*. London: George Allen & Unwin.

Steinhart, Edward I. (2006) *Black Poachers, White Hunters*. Oxford: James Currey.

Stoneham, C.T. (n.d., c.1934) *Hunting Wild Beasts with Rifle and Camera*. London: Thomas Nelson & Sons.

Thompson, Gerald and Oxford Scientific Films (1981) *Focus on Nature*. London: Faber & Faber.

van Dyke, W.S. (1931) *Horning into Africa*. Stationers' Hall and privately printed by California Graphic Press.

van Lawick, Hugo (1977) *Savage Paradise*. London: Wm. Collins & Harvill Press.

van Lawick, Hugo (1973) *Solo, the Story of an African Wild Dog*. London: Collins.

Vidal, John (2002) 'Shoot to thrill', *Guardian*, 16 October.

Watt, Harry (1951) 'Where no vultures fly', in *Everybody's Weekly*, 10 November, pp 28–9.

Whiteman, Lily (1997) 'Violence, lies and videotape: wildlife film making takes a few liberties with the truth', *Environmental Magazine*.

Willock, Colin (1978) *The World of Survival*. London: Andre Deutsch.

Willock, Colin (1981) 'The background of "Survival" and the making of wildlife programmes for television', *BKSTS Journal*, September.

Willock, Colin (1991) *Wildfight – A History of Conservation*. London: Jonathan Cape.

Appendix

Chronology of Wildlife Filmmaking in East Africa

This list is by no means complete, but I include it for interest and so that there is a basis upon which other people can expand. While I have tried to stick to films made in Kenya, I have also included films made in East Africa generally because they were made by people mentioned in the text. All of my 'big five' worked in areas other than Kenya, and Viewfinders also handled projects in neighbouring countries in the early years. The old films such as Africa Speaks and Trader Horn covered Kenya, Tanzania, Uganda, and what was then the Congo, when the borders were not where they are today, if there were any at all.

I have included a number of feature films, because they included animals – many of them tame, and provided by my uncle-in-law, Tom Carr Hartley.

Compiling this list has not been easy. The Kenya National Archives do not have a list of films in their possession, nor any comprehensive records of films that have been made. The Ministry of Information's Film Department can only give me inaccurate records from the year 2003 – previous records appear to have been destroyed. I have therefore had to rely on the memories of friends, family, local historians, stills photographers, professional hunters and safari guides, conservationists, journalists, vets, animal trainers, my own film archive, and of course the filmmakers themselves. Kearton, the Johnsons, Hoefler, the Denises and others wrote books about their experiences, and there are a number of biographies on some of the key people – these are all listed in the bibliography. I have been in email contact with people all over the globe and am very grateful to them for sharing their memories and their knowledge. Any misinterpretations or inaccuracies are my own.

Date	Details
1863	First photo of an African animal (dead), on a dry glass plate, by Prof. Fritsch
1871	Cherry Kearton born
1888	Monsieur Coillard had filming equipment when hunting with F. Selous
1890	Edward North Buxton started to photograph as alternative to hunting
1896	Unnamed photographer with 3rd Baron Delamere's expedition to East Africa
1900	Harry Johnston considered photography to be the sportsmanship of the future: 'If I had my way I would present a telephoto camera instead of a rifle to the US President.'
1900	Pop Binks arrived in Kenya
1903	First professional photographic safari, C.G. Schillings (*Flashlights in the Jungle* book)
1904	Newland & Tarlton formed
1905	William Young set up photo studio in Nairobi
905	HK (Pop) Binks set up photo studio in Nairobi ((business burned in 1945/6)
1906	Charles J. Jones: *Lion Hunt*
1907	Dr Ad David from Switzerland. Safari along the Dinder river in Ethiopia – claimed to be first moving pictures shot in Africa.
1907	Mary Hall became the first woman to repeat Ewart Grogan's trek from Cape to Cairo
1907	Winston Churchill at Soysambu with Delamere (pig sticking)
1909	Cherry Kearton's first African safari to Kenya, with James L. Clark of the American Museum of Natural History. In August, filmed Theodore Roosevelt in Nyeri *TR in Africa*
1909	Colliers' Weekly magazine expedition?
1909	W.D. Boyce 'balloonograph' expedition with cameraman George Lawrence. Not a success.
1909	*Native Lion Hunt*, Cherry Kearton
1910	C.G. Schillings book *Camera Adventures in the African Wilds* with Dugmore and Clark
1910	Dr David filmed elephant hunts by the Shilluk, Dinka and Bari people along the White Nile
1910	Kearton also films Carl Hagenbeck collecting safari (Boma Trading Co)
1910	Carl Akeley hires some Nandi to stage a lion spearing ritual. Over 3 weeks, 14 lions and 5 leopards killed for him to get the footage. But his Urban bioscope camera inadequate, and footage never publicly screened. He started designing the Akeley camera.

1910	Kearton's film *Roosevelt in Africa* opens in New York
1910	*Lassooing Wild Animals in Africa* aka *The last of the Plainsmen*. Assist. Camera William David Gobbett
1911	Cherry Kearton returns to Kenya and meets Buffalo Jones
1911	Cherry Kearton *A Primitive Man's Career to Civilisation*
1911	Paul Rainey filmed in Laisamis with Pop Binks, John Hemment and Carl Akeley + ? Lydford. *The Waterhole*, first major film.
1911	Paul Rainey, John Hemment, Pop Binks: *Scenes of African Animals*
1912	Paul Rainey invited to Soysambu by Delamere
1912	Paul J Rainey's *African Hunt*. Camera J.C. Hemment/Pop Binks. Some footage may have been bought from Carl Akeley, showing safari preparations, hunting with dogs, wildlife at a waterhole.
1912/13	Andy Anderson & Jim Sutherland + 2 US cameramen, Luperte and Hargon wanted to film elephant charging.
1913	Vehicles arrived in Kenya
1913	Cherry Kearton's African films screened in New York in May, introduced by Theodore Roosevelt.
1914	First underwater film: Ernest Williamson, USA, *30,000 Leagues under the Sea*.
1914	*Common beasts of Africa* and *Rainey's African Hunt*. Paul J. Rainey – possibly recycled footage from his 1912 film, plus some footage from 1909–10 which was bought.
1914	*Military Drill of the Kikuyu*, filmed by Carl Akeley, for Paul Rainey. Includes leopard and cheetahs.
1914–19	*With Eustace in Africa* filmed between 1914–18 by Harry K. Eustace.
1915	*Lady MacKenzie's Big Game Pictures*, camera Harold Sintzenich. Lady Grace MacKenzie on safari. Also called *Heart of Africa*.
1915	*In the Midst of African Wilds*, Selig Polyscope Co., Lloyd B. Carleton, Emma Bell (not filmed in Africa).
1915–16	Cherry Kearton did military service in Kajiado
1916	Carl Akeley patents the Akeley camera
1919–22	Hunting Big Game in Africa with Gun and Camera, H.A. Snow and son Sidney shot 125,000 feet of film. Ran for 3 months at New York Lyric Theatre. Carl Akeley denounced it for misrepresenting Africa, and for faking some scenes.
1921	Swedish cameraman Oskar Olson films lions near the Mara river.
1921	Carl Akeley films gorillas on an American Museum of Natural History trip with Herbert Bradley. First pictures of gorillas in the wild. Called *Meandering in Africa*.
1921	*Jungle Adventures* – Martin Johnson travelogue with wildlife scenes

1921	*Wild Men of Africa*	Leonard J. Vandenbergh
1921	Cherry Kearton filmed General Northey at Fort Jesus	
1921–2	*Meandering in Africa*	Carl Akeley
1922–4	William J Morden expedition (ethnographic)	Camera Herford Tynes Cowling, shot on 16mm
1923	*Elephants of Kenya's North Country*	
1923	*On the Equator*	Cherry Kearton
1923	*Trailing African Wild Animals*	Martin and Osa Johnson. 7 lions, 4 black rhinos, an elephant, buffalo and antelope are shot. Film endorsed by American Museum of Natural History, and then Governor of Pennsylvania, Gifford Pinchot.
1923	*Roughest Africa*	Dir. Ralph Ceder. Laurel & Hardy
1924	The Johnsons with AMNH funding set out to make 3 films, none of which were completed when they returned in 1928.	
1924	*Equatorial Africa: Roosevelt's Hunting Grounds.*	Camera A.J. Klein. Travelogue from Kenya to Uganda and the Nile. Lion spearing footage also used in Johnson's *Simba*.
1925	*Cape to Cairo*	filmed by T.A. Glover, Court Treatt.
1925	Wildlife stills photographer A.R. Dugmore starts filming at Ngorongoro, including an elephant charge.	
1926	*Carl and Mary in Africa*	Filmed during the Eastman-Pomeroy-Akeley East Africa expedition. Includes camp scenes at Lukenya, also Uganda.
?1926	*With Cherry Kearton in the Jungle*	
1926	*Gorilla Hunt.*	Ben Burridge leads an attempt to capture gorillas. 1 elephant and 3 lions shot on camera.
1927	*Through Darkest Africa, in Search of White Rhinoceros*	Harry J Eustace (hunting film).
1927	*Into the Blue*	Martin and Osa Johnson lecture film, essentially a preview of the film *Simba*, from their footage at Marsabit.
1928	*West of Zanzibar* (silent)	Dir. Tod Browning. Lon Chaney, Lionel Barrymore
1928	Release of the Johnson's *Simba* (AMNH funding). Includes staged confrontations, provoked behaviour, dramatic events.	

Cobbled together from the 3 unfinished films they set out to make in 1924. Includes footage from Al J. Klein's *Equatorial Africa, Roosevelt's Hunting Grounds* which was purchased for $30,000. Includes the 1926 lion-spearing footage co-filmed by Carl Akeley, and a similar scene filmed by Klein. Several sound and silent versions released.

1928	*Adventuring Johnsons.*	2 reel silent lecture film
1928–9	*Africa Speaks.*	Paul Hoefler films the Colorado African Expedition from East to West Africa, safari organised by Mike Cottar. First colour documentary
1929	The Johnsons, with financial backing from Fox Film Corp. set out to film *Congorilla* – with sound.	
1929	*Up the Congo*	camera Charles Bell, dir. Alice O'Brien – travelogue.
1929	*Wild Heart of Africa*	camera Kenneth Walker, dir. Cub Walker. Expedition of Walker-Arbuthnot African expedition from Egypt south.
1930	*Three Boy Scouts in Africa.*	Martin & Osa Johnson, lecture film
1930	*Across the World with Mr & Mrs Johnson*	Camera Russell Shields, dir. J. Leo Meehan. Sound feature.
1930	*Boru, the Ape Boy*	Dir. Major C Court Treatt
1930	*Blizzard on the equator*	Carveth Wells. Efforts by Wells to debunk myths of animals' man-eating savagery
1930	*Tembi*	Cherry Kearton
1930	*Dassan*	Cherry Kearton's film about penguins, off the South African coast. He appears and speaks on camera for the first time.
1931	*Trader Horn*	Dir. W.S. van Dyke, starring Harry Carey, Edwina Booth
1932	*Red Dust*	Clark Gable & Jean Harlow. Later remade as *Mogambo*
1932	*Tarzan, the Ape Man*	Johnny Weismuller. Dir. W.S. van Dyke
1932	*Congorilla*	Johnsons playing 'stars' but some set-up wildlife footage. Sound feature.
1933	*Taming the Jungle*	Paul D Wyman
1933	*Untamed Africa*	Wynant G Hubbard's film of a family safari, released by Warners
1934	*Tarzan and his Mate*	Dir. Cedric Gibbons

1934	*Wings over Africa*	Johnsons silent lecture film
1935	*Giants and Pygmies*	Armand Denis
1935	*Baboona*	Wildlife film but with many captive animals. Martin & Osa Johnson
1935–6	*Austrian Motorcycle Expedition through Africa: Cape Town to Cairo,*	Josef & Hilde Bohmer
1936	*Jungle Jim* (serial)	Dir. Ford Beebe & Clifford Smith
1936	*Tarzan escapes*	Dir. Richard Thorpe
1937	*King Solomon's Mines*	Dir. Robert Stevenson. Paul Robeson
1937	*Children of Africa*	Martin & Osa Johnson, filmed between 1924–8
1937	Martin Johnson dies in plane crash near LA	
1937	*African Holiday*	Harry Pearson travelogue with wildlife footage
1938	*Dark Rapture*	Armand Denis safari film (Belgian Congo) 20th Century Fox
1938	William D. Campbell African Expedition	Trip to Uganda, Congo, and Sudan but started in Nyeri, Kenya
1938	*Jungles Calling*	silent lecture film (Osa Johnson)
1938	Harry Snyder East Africa expedition	A collecting trip for AMNH, filmed at Voi, Taita, Lake Jipe before proceeding to Tanzania
1938	Cherry Kearton returned to Outspan where he had filmed TR	
1939	*Tarzan Finds a Son*	Dir. Richard Thorpe
1939	*Stanley and Livingstone*	Dir. Henry King. Spencer Tracy, Nancy Kelly, Richard Greene. Osa Johnson as consultant
1939	Hans Hass' first u/w film	
1940	*I Married Adventure*	Compilation of the Johnson's films based on Osa's ghost-written book of the same name.
1940	Cherry Kearton died outside the BBC	
1941	*African Paradise*	silent lecture film (Osa Johnson)
1941	*Tarzan's Secret Treasure*	Dir. Richard Thorpe
1941	*Jungle Girl* (series)	Dir. William Witney & John English
1942	*Tarzan's New Adventure*	Dir. Richard Thorpe
1947	*Journey to Adventure: a film chronicle of Cherry Kearton*	BBC
1947	William J. Morden expedition	Pastoral people of North West Kenya, Turkana

1948	AMNH Central African Expedition (James L. Clark)	Birds, mammals, insects, also Maasai and Nandi people. Camped at Narok before moving to Uganda and Congo
1948	23 November, Armand & Michaela Denis married in Potosi	
1949	*Savage Splendour*	Armand Denis safari filmLewis Cotlow + David Denis (son)
1950	*King Solomon's Mines*	Dir. Compton Bennett & Andrew Marton Stewart Granger, Deborah Kerr. Michaela Denis as Kerr's double. Academy award for best colour photography.
1950	Osa Johnson's *Big Game Hunt*	Old footage recut into 26 half hour tv shows.
1950	*Jungle Stampede*	Dir. George Breakston
1950	*Wakamba* (fictional film with much wildlife footage)	Edgar M Queeny African expedition for AMNH
1950	*Wandorobo* (first footage of honeyguide's relationship with man). Filmed in the Mara.	Edgar M Queeny African expedition for AMNH
1950	*The Road to Nairobi*	Jack Benny, Bob Hope, Jerry Lewis, Dean Martin
1951	Serengeti National Park formed	
1951	Marlin Perkins and Don Meier film on 16mm with sound establishing the model for the series *Wild Kingdom* (which remained a studio based series).	
1951	*African Queen*	Spencer Tracy, Katherine Hepburn. Dir. John Huston
1951	*Where No Vultures Fly*	filmed in Tsavo, starring Anthony Steele, Dinah Sheridan and William Simons, Ealing Studios/African Film Productions. Based on Mervyn Cowie's book (which was NOT called Ivory Trader)
1952	*Snows of Kilimanjaro*	Dir. Henry King. Gregory Peck, Susan Hayward, Ava Gardner
1952	*Tembo*	Dir. Howard Hill
1952	*Champagne Safari*	Aly Khan/Rita Hayworth
1952	*Bwana Devil* (aka *Lions of Gulu*)	Dir. Arch Oboler starring Robert Stack, Barbara Britton, Ramsay Hill
1952	Jacques Cousteau's first colour film	
1953	May. First wildlife programme on British television. Peter Scott live OB from Slimbridge. *Severn Wildfowl*	
1953	Armand and Michaela Denis make their first appearance on TV in England (October)	

1953	RSPB film unit set up	
1953	*Mogambo*	Dir. John Ford. Clark Gable, Ava Gardner, Grace Kelly, Donald Sinden
1953	7 January	Osa Johnson died of a heart attack
1953	*Below the Sahara*	Armand Denis safari film Camera Tom Stobart
1953	*Maasailand*	Edgar M Queeny/AMNH African Expedition 1953. Filmed in Narok district. Much wildlife footage, plus Maasai eunoto creemony.
1953	*Stronghold of the Wild*	Dir. Jack Swaine
1954	*Wild Birds and Man*	CBS/AMNH Adventure TV series. Used E.M. Queeny's footage of honeyguide in the Mara, shot in 1950.
1954	*Africa Adventure*	Dir. Robert Ruark. Photog. Harry Selby & Andrew Holmberg
1954	*Filming Wild Animals*	Armand and Michaela Denis series starts on 11 November, BBC
1954	*Operation Rhino*	Dir. Tom Mann for Anglia. (Ken Randall, Pat O'Connell, Lou Wedd)
1954	*Manyatta*	Armand Denis (Des Bartlett)
1954	*We Capture a Baby Elephant*	Armand Denis (Des Bartlett)
1954	*Thirst in Elephant Country*	Armand Denis (Des Bartlett)
1954	*Romantic Wajir*	Armand Denis (Des Bartlett)
1954	*At home with the Lions*	Armand Denis (Des Bartlett)
1954	*Toto and the Poachers*	World Safari Productions. Henry Geddes. Dir. Brian Salt
1954	*Safari to Adventure*	Armand Denis (Des Bartlett)
1955	*African Safari*	AMNH Chairman and curator Harold E. Anthony, and Charles Collingwood on safari. Includes clips from the Johnsons' *Simba* and Armand Denis' *Below the Sahara*.
1955	Jan. Heinz Sielmann's woodpecker film first shown	
1955	*Minnie's Babies*	Armand Denis (Des Bartlett)
1955	*The Wells of Buna*	Armand Denis (Des Bartlett)
1955	*Zanzabuku*	Prod. Lewis Cotlow *(aka Dangerous Safari)* camera Freddy Ford, David Mason
1955	*The African Lion*	A Disney adventure, filmed by Al and Elma Milotte, dir. James Algar. Disney. Tanzania, Kenya, Kruger

1955	*Look* premières in September on BBC	Peter Scott
1955	*Diving to Adventure* premières	Hans Hass
1955	ITV launched	
1955	Marlin Perkins here filming *Zoo Parade*, to become *Wild Kingdom*	
1956	The Morden African Expedition 1956	Hunting expedition in Nairobi, Isiolo, NFD, Marsabit, Mt Kenya, Amboseli, Magadi
1956	Leni Riefenstahl arrived Nairobi en route to Somalia (car accident)	
1956	*On Safari – The Egg and the Snake*	DoY school, Denises, Des Bartlett, Alan Root
1956	*Kinship of the Creature*	Mercury Film Productions
1956	*Beyond Mombasa*	Dir. George Marshall. Cornel Wilde, Donna Reed, Christopher Lee
1956	*Kein Platz für wilde Tiere (No Place for Wildlife)*	Bernard Grzimek's film criticising safari hunting
1956	*Elsa and Her Cubs*	Joy Adamson lecture film, Benchmark Productions
	Ein Platz für Tiere (A Place for Animals)	Bernard Grzimek's live animal TV show on German TV. Includes sequences filmed by his son Michael, Heinz Sielmann and others
1956	*Look*	Peter Scott in Kenya
1956	*Odongo, an Adventure of the African Frontier*	Warwick Films, Dir. John Gilling
1956	*Dunlop Safari*	Armand Denis (Des Bartlett)
1957	BBC Natural History Unit (NHU) formed	
1957	*The Dying Plains of Africa: the poaching problem*	Armand Denis (Des Bartlett, Alan Root, Hugo van Lawick, Ted Davis)
1957	*The Dying Plains of Africa: drought*	Armand Denis (Des Bartlett, Alan Root, Hugo van Lawick, Ted Davis)
1957	*Tarzan*	(Thika), Gordon Scott
1957	*Something of Value*	Dir. Richard Brooks, starring Rock Hudson, Sidney Poitier
1957	*Naked Africa*	Dir. Ray Phoenix
1957	*Woman and the Hunter (Triangle on Safari)*	Phoenix Productions, George Breakston
1957	*African Patrol*	John Bentley, George Breakston (39 episodes)
1958	*On Safari*	Armand and Michaela Denis, premières on the BBC
1958	*On Safari – Capturing Giraffe*	Denises and Des Bartlett

1958	*On Safari – The Search for Gertie*	Amboseli, Denises and Des Bartlett
1958	*On Safari – off the Beaten Track*	Armand Denis (Des Bartlett)
1958	*On Safari – Search for the Big Tuskers*	Armand Denis (Des Bartlett)
1958	*On Safari – They Fly by Twilight*	*Armand Denis (Des Bartlett)*
1958	*The Baboon Laughed*	Kenya Productions Ltd
1958	*Shooting Star*	Kenya Productions Ltd
1958	*Flamingos with Leslie Brown*	BBC, *Look*
1959	*The Reluctant Mermaid*	Carr Hartley Film Productions, director/producer Tom Mann, camera Fred Ford Jr, Jim Marshall
1959	*Jungle Boy*	Dir. George Breakston. Mike Carr Hartley
1959	*Serengeti Shall Not Die*	Bernard Grzimek, Okapia Films. Filmed by Michael Grzimek and Alan Root. Wins OSCAR academy award for best documentary feature.
1959	*And So – We Went to Africa*	David and Barbara Lowry safari to Kenya and Tanzania. Cameraman Allen Bendig. Shot in Garba Tula, Amboseli. Excellent wildlife footage
1960	*Elsa the Lioness*	BBC David Attenborough
1960	*Snows of Kilimanjaro*	Robert Ryan, Ann Todd
1960	Joy Adamson's book *Born Free* published	
1960	*My Friends the Wild Chimpanzees*	National Geographic lecture film, Hugo van Lawick
1960	*The Elephant that Walked on Air*	Okapia Films, Bernard Grzimek, Alan Root
1961	*Hatari*	John Wayne, Hardy Kruger, Elsa Martinelli, Red Buttons. Dir. Howard Hawks
1961	BBC introduced colour	
1961	*SOS Rhino (Bolt from the Blue)*	Survival, John Buxton, Alan Root
1961	*The Last Rhino*	feature, Henry Geddes of World Safari Productions/ CFF Productions
1961	*On Safari – Flamingos*	Armand Denis (Des Bartlett)
1961	*On Safari – World of Termites*	Armand Denis (Des Bartlett)
1961	*On Safari – We Catch a Crocodile*	Armand Denis (Des Bartlett)
1961	*On Safari – Njemps*	Armand Denis (Des Bartlett)
1961	*On Safari – Saving the Rhino*	Armand Denis (Des Bartlett)
1961	*Wild Gold: East Africa, a land in crisis*	For AWF. Filmed by JR Simon (ex-Disney)

1962	*Balloon from Zanzibar*	BBC, Alan Root
1962	*On Safari – Around Our Garden*	Armand Denis (Des Bartlett)
1962	*On Safari – We Catch a Python*	Armand Denis (Des Bartlett)
1962	*On Safari – Frogs and Lizards*	Armand Denis (Des Bartlett)
1962	*On Safari – World of the Wasps*	Armand Denis (Des Bartlett)
1962	*On Safari – Our Camp at Crescent Island*	Armand Denis (Des Bartlett)
1962	*On Safari – The Herons of Nairobi*	Armand Denis (Des Bartlett)
1962	*On Safari – Big Game Darting*	Armand Denis (Des Bartlett)
1962	*Robert Stack: Lions*	ABC American Sportsman
1962	*Jimmy Doolittle: rhino, leopard, elephant, buffalo*	ABC American Sportsman
1962	*Flamingos at Magadi*	Alan Root
1962	*Animal Magic* Starts on BBC	Johnny Morris
1962	Marsabit made a national park	
1963	*The Lion*	William Holden, Trevor Howard, Bill Ryan. Dir. Jack Cardiff. Animal trainer Ralph Helfer
1963	BBC NHU first colour film on TV	
1963	*The Pearl in the Desert*	Alan Root
1963	*Call Me Bwana*	Bob Hope, Dir. Gordon Douglas
1963	*On Safari – The Lioness*	Armand Denis (Simon Trevor)
1963	*On Safari – Maasai*	Armand Denis (Des Bartlett)
1963	*On Safari –Operation Antelope*	Armand Denis (Des Bartlett)
1963	*On Safari –Treetops' visitors*	Armand Denis (Des Bartlett)
1963	*Rothschild Giraffe/Menengai*	Bernard Grzimek, Alan Root
1963	*The New Ark*	Survival for WWF, Alan Root
1963	Canadian Broadcasting *The Nature of Things* starts	
1963	*Miss Jane Goodall and the Wild Chimpanzees*	1st National Geographic wildlife film, aired on PBS. Hugo van Lawick
1963	*Return Safari*	Shaw Films, Alan Root
1963	*Pity the Poor Crocodile*	Survival, Alan Root
1964	*The Permanent Way*	For EARH, Caltex. Dir. Hal Moray
1964	*Cowboy in Africa*	Starring Chuck Connors, Tom Nardini, Ronald Howard. Dir Ivan Tors, Camera Simon Trevor
1964	*The Birds*	Survival, Alan Root
1964	*Give a Dog a Name*	Survival, Alan Root

1964	The Last Safari	Dir. Henry Hathaway. 3rd Unit Simon Trevor
1964	Daktari	Dir. Ivan Tors. Kenya scenes filmed by Simon Trevor
1965	Life is for Living	(animal catching) Dir. Claude Lalouche, Tz
1965	Frank & Helen Schreider Safari	National Geographic, Bob Campbell
1965	A Price on their Heads	Survival, Alan Root
1965	Hell's Gate	Survival, Alan Root
1966	The Walking Birds	Simon Trevor
1966	Dr Leakey and the Dawn of Man	National Geographic, dir./camera Guy Blanchard
1966	Born Free	feature based on Joy Adamson's (1960) book, James Hill
1966	Bird Shooting (Sandgrouse)	ABC American Sportsman, with Phil Harris and Bing Crosby
1966	A tear for Karamoja	Survival Alan Root
1967	Africa	ABC, four hour special(Bob Campbell)
1967	The Lions are Free	Swan Productions (dir. James Hill). Documentary starring Bill Travers & Virginia McKenna about Boy and Girl
1967	Africa, Texas Style	TV series based on Cowboy in Africa. John Mills, Hugh O'Brien. Dir. Andrew Marton
1967	Flamingos with Leslie Brown	BBC Look
1967	Kill by Kindness	Survival, Alan Root
1967	The Last Safari	Stewart Grainger. Dir. Henry Hathaway
1968	Leopard Relocation	ABC American Sportsman, with Patrick O'Neill
1968	Guinea Fowl	ABC American Sportsman, Bing Crosby and Phil Harris
1968	Iain DH and Boadicea	? Bob Campbell
1968	The Birth of Man	National Geographic promotional lecture, Bob Campbell
1968	East Lake Rudolf Expedition	National Geographic promotional lecture, Bob Campbell
1968	OSF formed	
1968	The Forest is our Friend	Filmed by Dick Thomsett for the Office of Information
1968	Bill Ryan, Hunter on Wheels	BBC
1969	Mzima, Portrait of a Spring	Alan Root for BBC World About Us

1969	*Nothing Going On*	Survival, Alan Root
1969	*Roan Translocation*	ABC American Sportsman starring Joe Kennedy
1969	*Buffalo Hunt*	ABC American Sportsman starring Wally Shirra (astronaut)
1969	*Photo Safari and Bird Shoot*	ABC American Sportsman, starring George Plimpton
1969	*Nile Perch at Lake Turkana*	ABC American Sportsma, starring Gene Kelly & Doug Sanders
1969	*The Killing Game*	BBC
1969	*An Elephant Called Slowly*	Morning Star Productions, Dir James Hill. Simon Trevor
1970	*African Journey*	Dir. George Bloomfield.
1970	*African Seafari*	BBC *World About Us*, Dir. Ned Kelly (BBC)
1970	*Baobab*	Alan Root for BBC *World About Us*
1970	*The Way of the Wild*	Caledonian Films, Dick Thomsett for the EA Wildlife Society
1970	*Pippa, the story of Joy Adamson and a cheetah.*	Dir. Kenneth Talbot for London Weekend Television International.
1971	*The African Elephant* (aka *King Elephant*)	Simon Trevor. Nominated for Oscar
1971	*The Hellstrom Chronicles*	Wolper Productions, Simon Trevor
1971	*Kifaru*	MGM for BBC World about us (scientist John Goddard, Tsavo) producer Nick Noxon
1971	*Box me a Bongo*	Alan Root for BBC
1971	*Kenya's Heritage*	Government of Kenya for the travel trade
1971	*Monkeys, Apes and Man*	National Geographic Special. Gorillas filmed by Bob Campbell. Prod. Denis Kane
1971	*The Lion at World's End*	Morning Star productions (dir Bill Travers & James Hill). Some filmed by Simon Trevor
1971	*Living Free*	Dir. Jack Couffer. Nigel Davenport, Susan Hampshire
1971	*The Darwin Adventure*	Jack Couffer (one sequence filmed at Baringo)
1971	*Ahmed*	ABC American Sportsman, with John Huston
1971	*Kenya National Parks*	ABC American Sportsman, with Gloria Stewart

1971	*Roan Translocation*	ABC American Sportsman, with Joe Kennedy
1971	*Elephant Country*	Ivan Tors, using Simon Trevor out takes
1971	*Wings over the Rift*	Survival
1971	15 August	Armand Denis died
1972	*Jane Goodall and the World of Animal Behaviour*, aired in US.	Filmed by Hugo van Lawick
1972	*Great Parks of the World: Nairobi*	BBC Richard Brock
1972	*The Stouts in Africa*	Gardner and Clare Stout, filming trip. Shimba Hills, Tsavo, Samburu, Nakuru. Good wildlife footage
1972	*The Biggest Bongo in the World* (aka *The track of the African Bongo*).	Dir Frank Zuniga, Disney
1972	*Solo, the Story of an African Wild Dog*	Hugo van Lawick
1972	*Man of the Serengeti (George Schaller)*	National Geographic, Alan Root
1972	*Christian the Lion*	Morning Star Productions. Prod. Will Travers. Camera Simon Trevor
1972	*The Man of the Maasai*	BBC
1972	*Around the World in 80 Minutes*	BBC *World About Us*, Richard Brock
1972	*Adventure in Africa with George Plimpton*	Starring George Plimpton. Simon Trevor
1973	*Trader Horn*	Dir. Reza S Badivi. Rod Taylor, Anne Haywood
1973	17 January	Ahmed the elephant died
1973	*Omo River Run*	Bob Campbell/Alan Root
1973	*The Floating Worlds of Naivasha*	Survival, Cindy Buxton
1973	Australian Broadcasting NHU set up	
1973	*Web of Life: the living mountains*	BBC *World About Us*
1973	*Web of Life: the living lakes*	BBC *World About Us*
1973	*Web of Life: the living savannah*	BBC *World About Us*
1973	*Man, a New Perspective*	National Geographic lecture, Richard Leakey
1973	*Serengeti Has Not Died*	Survival, Alan Root for TANAPA
1973	*Travels Through the Northern Frontier District of Kenya*	AMNH, Water G Dyer and Betty Dyer
1974	Partridge Films formed	
1974	*The Big Cats*	National Geographic TV special. Alan Root +
1974	*Born Free* TV series	Camera Jack Couffer

1974	*The Baboons of Gombe*	BBC *World About Us*, Hugo van Lawick
1974	*Wilderness: Lake Rudolf*	BBC *World About Us*, Ned Kelly, Jack Bellamy
1974	*The Voyage of the Mir-el-lah*	Survival Bob Campbell
1974	*Wild Dogs of Africa*	Hugo van Lawick
1974	*Search for the Great Apes*	Gorilla section Bob Campbell (Rwanda)
1974	*Among the Elephants* (aka *The Family that Lives with Elephants and We Live with Elephants*)	Survival Dieter Plage
1974	*Bones of Contention*	Survival Bob Campbell
1974	*Africa, Forest or Desert?*	Simon Trevor for WWF
1974	*Visit to a Chief's Son*	Producer Robert Halmi. Simon Trevor
1974	*The Year of the Wildebeest*	Survival Alan Root
1974	*The Silent Sky*	
1975	*Bill's Big Hill* (series *Taste for Adventure*)	BBC Richard Brock. Bill Woodley, Mt Kenya
1975	*There are Warthogs at the Bottom of my Garden*	Survival Bob Campbell
1975	*The Hyena Story*	BBC *World About Us*, Hugo van Lawick
1975	*Safari by Balloon*	Survival (Dieter Plage, Bob Campbell, Alan Root)
1975	Lee Lyon Killed by Elephant in Rwanda	
1975	*The End of the Game*	Opus films, Dir. Robin Lehman
1975	*What Use is Wildlife*	BBC *World About Us*, Richard Brock
1975	*The Ivory Poachers*	Simon Trevor for Wildlife Clubs of Kenya
1976	*Kenworthy's Kenya*	BBC, dir. George Inger
1976	*The Day of the Zebra*	BBC *World About Us* (John Sparks, Maurice Tibbles), Samburu/Tanzania
1976	*On the Track of Rare Animals (Sokoke)*	BBC *World About Us*, Richard Brock
1976	*Poaching*	ABC American Sportsman with George Plimpton. Simon Trevor
1976	*Messengers of the Gods*	Survival Bob Campbell
1976	*The Parenthood Game*	Survival Bob Campbell
1976	*Lions of the Serengeti*	BBC *World About Us*, Hugo van Lawick
1977	*Wildlife on One* starts	BBC
1977	*The Elephant Run*	BBC *World About Us* (camera Mo Dhillon)

1977	*The Dusts of Kilimanjaro*	Survival Bob Campbell
1977	*Land of the Maasai*	Survival Bob Campbell
1977	*El Molo, Hippo Hunters of the Jade Sea*	Mohamed Amin
1977	*The Mysterious Plague*	Survival Bob Campbell
1977	*Run Cheetah Run*	BBC Wildlife on One. Stanley Joseph (filmed in Amboseli)
1977	*How Green Is My Quarry?*	Survival Bob Campbell
1977	*Last Kingdom of the Elephants*	Survival Bob Campbell and Cindy Buxton
1977	*Hunters of the Plains*	Survival Bob Campbell (finished John Pearson's film)
1977	Leni Riefenstahl learned to dive at Driftwood Club in Malindi, aged 72	
1978	*Bloody Ivory*	BBC *World About Us* Simon Trevor
1978	*Survival in the Air*	Survival, Alan Root, Dieter Plage
1978	*Rivers of Sand*	Survival Simon Trevor
1978	*Africa's Tallest Story*	BBC *World About Us* Barry Paine, Hugh Maynard Tanzania
1978	*In the Footsteps of Cherry Kearton*	BBC
1978	*Mud, Mud, Glorious Mud*	Survival, Cindy Buxton, Lee Lyon, Bob Campbell
1978	*The Tallest Story*	Survival Bob Campbell
1978	*Messengers of the Gods*	Survival Bob Campbell
1978	*Castles of Clay*	Survival Alan Root
1978	*Last Chance for the Grevy?*	BBC Wildlife on One Adrian Warren
1978	*Shirley Strum and the Pumphouse Gang*	Survival Bob Campbell
1978	*The Fastest Thing on Four Legs*	Survival Bob Campbell
1979	*Life on Earth*	BBC mega series, several sequences
1979	*Mistress of the Apes*	Jenny Newmann, Dir. Larry Buchanan
1979	*Wildlife Moving Picture Show*	BBC *World About Us* Jeffrey Boswall
1979	*Rhino Capture at Solio*	BBC Brian Barron
1979	*The End of the Game*	ABC American Sportsman, Cheryl Tiegs & Peter Beard
1979	*The Last Giraffe* (with Betty Leslie Melville)	CBS Dir. Jack Couffer
1979	*Last Stand in Eden*	National Geographic TV Special + Iain Douglas Hamilton
1980	3 January	Joy Adamson murdered

1980	A Tale of Africa (aka Green Horizons, Afurika Monogatari)	Sanrio Films Japan. Director Susumu Hani, co-director Simon Trevor. Starred James Stewart, Philip Sayer
1980	The Joy Adamson Story	Camera Dick Thomsett
1980	The Greatest	Survival, Alan Root, Dieter Plage
1980	The Impossible Bird	BBC Wildlife on One Richard Brock, Hugh Miles
1980	Red River Safari	BBC Wildlife on One Richard Brock/ Hugh Miles
1980	Two in the Bush	Survival Alan Root. Sold in the US as Lights, Action, Africa
1981	Savage Harvest	Ralph Helfer + 100 animals from California
1981	The Flame Trees of Thika	TV series based on Elspeth Huxley book
1981	The Days of the Jackal	BBC, Dilys Breese, Hugh Maynard
1981	Birds of the Burning Soda	Survival Bob Campbell
1981	A Season in the Sun	Survival Alan Root
1981	Nature Watch: Jonathan Scott in the Mara	Director Robin Brown
1981	Symbiosis	65mm for Epcot Centre. Simon Trevor
1982	The Way of the Jackal	Survival Bob Campbell
1982	A Floating Home	Survival Cindy Buxton
1982	The Big Boss	Survival Bob Campbell
1982	Salute to the Serengeti	Survival, Alan Root
1982	Ambush at Maasai Mara	BBC Wildlife on One (Keenan Smart/ Hugh Miles)
1982	A Leap in the Dark	Survival, Alan Root
1982	Leakey's Wildlife Antenna	BBC2. Camera Mohinder Dhillon
1982	In the Footsteps of Elephants	Dir. Philippe de Brocca. Camera Simon Trevor
1983	No Laughing Matter	Survival Bob Campbell
1983	Among the Wild Chimpanzees	National Geographic, Hugo van Lawick
1983	Roger Whittaker in Kenya	Timbo Productions, dir. Tom Ingle & Roger Whittaker
1984	The Nairobi Affair	Charlton Heston
1984	The Living Planet	BBC mega series – several sequences
1984	Antelope, the Graceful Art of Success	Survival Bob Campbell
1984	The Rains Came	Survival Simon Trevor
1984	A Question of Space	BBC TNW Robin Hellier

1984	*The Walking Birds*	Survival Simon Trevor
1984	*No Laughing Matter*	Survival Bob Campbell
1984	*The Legend of the Lightning Bird*	Survival Alan Root
1984	*The African Experience*	BBC Zoo 2000
1984	*Tumblers in the Sky*	Survival Simon Trevor
1984	*Kitum, the Elephant Cave*	BBC Derek Bromhall
1984	*Two of a Kind*	Survival, Simon Trevor
1984	*The Meanest Animal in the World*	Survival, Simon Trevor
1985	*Out of Africa*	Dir. Sydney Pollack. Meryl Streep, Robert Redford. 2nd unit Simon Trevor
1985	*The Mystery of the Flying Worms*	Survival Bob Campbell
1985	*The Colour Purple*	Dir. Stephen Spielberg. 2nd unit wildlife filmed by Simon Trevor
1985	*Nature Special Report: Maasai Mara*	BBC
1985	*Birds of a Feather*	Survival Simon Trevor
1985	*Blue Peter Safari to Kenya*	BBC
1985	*Leopards of Kora*	Thames TV. Narrator Richard Widmark
1985	*King Solomon's Mines*	Richard Chamberlain
1985	*The Birds from Hades*	Survival Bob Campbell
1985	*Moving Day for the Pumphouse Gang*	Survival Bob Campbell
1986	*Daphne Sheldrick & the Orphans of Tsavo*	Survival Simon Trevor
1986	*Skyhunters*	BBC *The Natural World*, Dilys Breeze
1986	*Together They Stand*	Survival Simon Trevor
1986	*Kopjes: islands in a sea of grass*	Survival, Alan Root
1986	*The great African Safari Bird Rally*	BBC Adrian Warren
1986	*Leopard, a Darkness in the Grass*	BBC *The Natural World*, Hugh Miles
1986	*In the Shadow of Kilimanjaro*	Dir. Raju Patel. Timothy Bottoms, John Rhys-Davies
1986	*The Elephant Challenge*	BBC *The Natural World*, Robin Hellier
1986	*Drought of the Century*	Survival Simon Trevor
1986	*Solitary Confinement*	Survival, Alan Root
1986	*The Long African Day*	Survival
1987	*Kitchen Toto*	Harry Hook
1987	*Rhino*	
1987	*Father of the Lions*	KTCA
1988	*Lord of the Lions: George Adamson*	Yorkshire TV (Sandy Gall)

1988	The Great Rift: breaking the continent	
1988	The Great Rift: footprints in the valley	BBC The Natural World Adrian Warren
1988	The Great Rift: out of the ashes	
1988	The Bee Team	BBC Wildlife on One (bee-eaters) Alastair Fothergill
1988	People of the Forest	Partridge Films, Hugo van Lawick
1988	With Peter Beard in Africa: last word from paradise	Ndefu Productions, prod.Mel Stewart
1988	Elephants of Tsavo, Love & Betrayal	Survival Simon Trevor
1988	Shadow on the Sun	Stephanie Powers
1988	Rhino War	Pathfinder films Philip Cayford
1988	The Elephant Diary	
1988	The Secret Leopard	Richard Matthews
1988	The Long and the Short and the Tall	Survival: Bob Campbell
1988	Gorillas in the Mist	2nd unit in Kenya (Simon Trevor). Wildlife Alan Root. Consultant Bob Campbell
1989	Ivory Wars	Pathfinder films for BBC, Philip Cayford
1989	Crater of the Rain God	Zebra Films, Richard Matthews
1989	Supersense	John Downer Productions
1989	The Life and Legend of Jane Goodall	National Geographic
1989	Kenya Safari	Chile TV
1989	Lion of Africa	
1989	Echo of the Elephants	BBC The Natural World, Marian Zunz, John Sparks
1989	Mountains of the Moon	Dir. Bob Rafelso Patrick Bergin, Iain Glen, Richard E Grant
1989	Queen of the Beasts	Survival, Richard Matthews
1989	The Last Explorer (Wilfred Thesiger)	Robin Brown, Central TV for BBC
1989	Return to the Jade Sea	Chameleon Films, Dir. Chris Lister
1989	Elephant	National Geographic TV Special. Iain Douglas Hamilton
1989	20 August	George Adamson killed
1989	The Perfect Trip	Travel Channel. Dir. Mellen O'Keefe
1990	Kali the Lion	BBC, Simon King
1990	Trials of LIfe	BBC mega series
1990	Trees	CQFD Video

1990	*Cheetahs: the blood brothers*	Partridge Films, Hugo van Lawick
1990	*Can the Elephant be Saved?*	NOVA/Documentary Guild
1990	*The Tombs below Aruba*	Survival Simon Trevor
1990	*The Long Legged Marching Eagle*	Survival Barbara Tyack
1990	*The Last Tribe*	Joanne Sawicki
1990	*Maasai Mara*	
1990	*Here Be Dragons*	Survival, Alan Root
1990	*The Year of the Clouds*	Malone Gill Productions
1990	*White Hunter, Black Heart*	Feature with Clint Eastwood. 2nd Unit Simon Trevor
1990	*Africa: playing God with nature?*	National Geographic
1990	*Kilimanjaro*	Partridge Films
1990	*Blue Planet*	IMAX Toronto
1990	*A Fragile Alliance*	Ecoventures
1990	*Once More into the Termite Mound*	BBC (making of Trials of Life)
1990	*A Treeful of Birds*	Survival, Simon Trevor
1991	*Even the Animals Must Be Free*	BBC Peter Crawford
1991	*Soda Lakes*	BBC TNW
1991	*Africa's Cats: fight for survival*	American Adventure Productions
1991	*Running for Their Lives*	BBC TNW
1991	*The Haunted Huntress*	BBC Wildlife on One (cheetahs) Keith Scholey
1991	*Krokodile*	ZDF
1991	*Climbing Mt Kilimanjaro*	Partridge Films
1991	*Monkeys in the Mist*	Partridge Films
1991	*Super Predators*	Sable Enterprises
1991	*Mining for Madinah*	IPCA
1991	*Dry Country Specialists*	ZDF
1991	*Lifesense*	BBC, John Downer
1991	*The River*	Londolozi Productions
1991	*Green Blood*	Atico Asiete
1991	*Peter Beard/Douglas Hamiltons*	TamTam Productions
1991	*History of the Pumphouse Gang*	Canadian Broadcasting Corporation
1991	*Zebras, Patterns in the Grass*	
1991	*Fragile Earth: safari*	North South Productions for Ch.4/ Discovery. Producer Richard Keefe
1991	*The Horse with Stripes*	Cicada Films. Mike Herd

1991	*Mountain Gorillas*	Mt Gorilla Productions (IMAX) Dir. Adrian Warren
1991	*Keepers*	National Geographic
1991	*Dans les sillages de Henry M Stanley*	Atom Audiovisuelle
1991	*Sunlight & Shadow, the Dappled Cats*	Deeble and Stone for Survival
1991	*The Warthog and the Tea Bag*	BBC Richard Brock
1992	*Vets in the Wild, Hands on Lions*	BBC
1992	*Prisoners of the Sun: energy wars*	
1992	*Prisoners of the Sun: tight budgets*	BBC Keith Scholey
1992	*Prisoners of the Sun: fuel rations*	
1992	*Race for Life*	Partridge Films
1992	*Africa, the Serengeti*	Graphic Films (IMAX)
1992	*The River*	Londolozi Productions (Mara)
1992	*History of the Pumphouse Gang*	Survival, Bob Campbell
1992	*Kuki Gallman/wildlife art*	TamTam Productions
1992	*Turkana Expedition*	Italian TV
1992	*White Maasai*	Australia 60 minutes
1992	*Wildlife*	Nick Chevallier Productions
1992	*George Adamson, Born to Be Free*	Gareth Patterson
1992	*Pole to Pole*	Michael Palin
1992	*Velvet Claw*	BBC NHU Melinda Barker
1992	*Wildlife*	Zoo Life
1992	*Burn, Ivory, Burn*	Central Productions Robin Brown
1992	*Daphne Sheldrick's Orphans*	Turner Broadcasting
1992	*Wild Vets*	Lighthouse Films, Simon Normanton
1992	*Oh Elephant*	Video Now
1992	*African Wild Dogs: a tale of two sisters*	Partridge Films
1992	*Cheetah and Cubs in the Land of the Lions*	Partridge Films
1992	*African Wildlife*	Australia 60 minutes
1992	*Keepers of the Kingdom*	Discovery
1992	*Keepers of the Kingdom*	Survival Simon Trevor
1992	*Baboons*	National Geographic
1992	*Islands in the African Sky*	Partridge Films for BBC TNW (Patrick Morris, Alistair McEwen)
1993	*Echo of the Elephants, the Next Generation*	BBC TNW
1993	*Lions, Pride of Africa*	Partridge Films
1993	*Islands of Elephants*	American Adventure Productions

1993	*Hyena, the Great Opportunist*	Londolozi Productions
1993	*Caravan of Hope*	Afikim Productions
1993	*Water Harvesters*	Afikim Productions
1993	*Chimpanzees*	National Geographic
1993	*Lions*	Londolozi Productions
1993	*Firebird*	BBC TNW
1993	*The Private Life of Plants*	BBC mega series
1993	*A Graze with Danger*	BBC Owen Newman
1993	*Giraffe, the Impossible Animal*	BBC Sarah Byatt
1993	*A Tale of Two Crowns*	Living Planet Productions
1993	*Jumbos in the Clouds*	Living Planet Productions
1993	Dieter Plage dies in Sumatra	
1993	BBC *The World About Us* becomes *The Natural World*	
1993	*Endangered: crowned eagle, king of the forest*	Living Planet Productions
1993	*Endangered: crowned crane, queen of the marsh*	Living Planet Productions
1993	*In the Wild: lions with Anthony Hopkins*	Tigress Productions, Hugh Maynard
1993	*Warthogs, Hogging the Limelight*	BBC WOO
1993	*Velvet Claw*	BBC Melinda Barker
1993	*Reflections on Elephants*	National Geographic
1993	*The Floating Worlds of Lake Naivasha*	Survival: Cindy Buxton
1993	*Wild Dogs, a Tale of Two Sisters*	Partridge Films, Hugo van Lawick
1993	*Monkey in the Mirror*	BBC
1993	*The Year of the Jackal*	Partridge Films, Dave Houghton
1993	*The Mystery of the Flying Worms*	Survival Bob Campbell
1993	*Wildlife Crisis Campaign*	Element Foundation
1993	*Lake of the Flies*	Zebra Films Richard Matthews
1993	*Among the Baboons*	Canadian Broadcasting
1993	*Endangered: high & dry, a giraffe's view*	Living Planet Productions
1993	*Photo Safari*	ABC with James Brolin
1993	*Ape Man*	Granada
1994	*Gremlins of the Night*	BBC Wildlife on One bushbabies (Bernard Walton)
1994	*Born to Run*	Partridge Films, Sophie Buck
1994	*The Boy Shamaan*	John Downer Productions

1994	Flight over Africa	National Geographic
1994	The Valley of Our Ancestors	Café Productions
1994	Children's Science	BBC Schools
1994	To the Ends of the Earth	International Management
1994	Africa's Race for Life	Nature Conservation Films
1994	Wildlife Conservation	The Element Foundation
1994	Lions: pride in peril	Living Planet Productions
1994	Hot Hippo	BBC
1994	Natural Neighbours: elephants	BBC
1994	Natural Neighbours: pigs might fly	BBC
1994	Running Wild	Londolozi Productions
1994	Super Hunts	Londolozi Productions
1994	Nightmares of Nature: maneaters	Zebra Films
1994	Nightmares of Nature: squirm	Zebra Films
1994	Nightmares of Nature: in cold blood	Zebra Films
1994	The Lion's King	BBC Owen Newman
1994	Mara Nights	Ammonite Films, for BBC
1994	Marsabit, Where Eagles Dare to Fly	ZDF
1994	Besieged: war of the termites	BBC Andy Byatt
1994	Daphne Sheldrick's Orphans/Richard Leakey	Carte Blanche
1994	The Naked Eye	BBC
1994	Potted Histories	BBC
1994	Baby Animals	Wildsight Productions
1994	King George's Animals	Scorer Associates
1994	Gardeners in Eden	Scorer Associates
1994	Where Elephants Call Home	Scorer Associates
1994	Paradise in Trouble	Clive James
1994	Africa's Wildlife Warrior	Scorer Associates
1994	The Last Rhino?	Bellamy Productions
1994	Maximum Cheetah Velocity	Kreatures Productions
1994	Spots and Stripes Forever	Kreatures Productions
1994	Lion King Safari	Buena Vista Productions
1994	Wild Film	Partridge Films
1994	Flight Over the Equator	Beyond Productions
1994	Flight over Africa	National Geographic
1994	Hotshots	BBC, Simon King

1994	*Dances for Elephants*	Double Exposure
1994	*The Making of the Leopard Son*	Discovery
1994	*African Express*	
1994	*Born to Be Free*	George Adamson
1994	*Flight of the Rhino*	Encounters
1994	*The Hole Story*	Survival, Simon Trevor
1994	*After the Rains*	Survival, Simon Trevor
1995	*Flamingo watch*	BBC
1995	*Really Wild Show*	BBC Martyn Suker
1995	*Amboseli Elephants*	CBS 60 minutes
1995	*Warthogs, the Ivory Pigs*	ZDF
1995	*The Man who Saved the Animals*	Network First
1995	*Gorillas*	Green Umbrella
1995	*Project Life Lion*	Project Life Lion
1995	*Scientists at Work*	CBS 60 minutes
1995	*Campfire Safaris*	Fotoplus
1995	*Ostriches*	Partridge Films
1995	*Theme Park Promo*	Buena Vista Productions
1995	*Wings Over the Serengeti*	BBC/National Geographic
1995	*Dawn to Dusk* (Chimpanzees)	BBC
1995	*Global Sunrise*	BBC
1995	*Eyes in the Sky*	Stoneybrook Films for Discovery
1995	*Hippo Talk*	Paneikon SRL
1995	*The Marsh*	Londolozi Productions
1995	*African Love Story*	Bioscope Productions
1995	*Reputations: Joy Adamson – born wild?*	BBC London
1995	*Blue Peter*	BBC
1995	*Acacias and Bruchid Beetles*	Oxford Scientific Films
1995	*One in a Crowd*	Survival Anglia
1995	*Zebra, the Trailblazers*	BBC WOO Mike Richards
1995	*Primatologists*	Diverse Productions
1995	*The Lion's Share*	Nature Conservation Films/Discovery
1995	*The Lioness's Tale*	Nature Conservation Films
1995	*Baboons, too Close for Comfort*	Survival, Barbara Tyack
1995	*Predators: cheetah and leopard*	Survival, Caroline Brett
1995	*Predators: lion*	Survival, Caroline Brett

1995	*The Ghost and the Darkness*	New Era Productions (2nd unit Jack Couffer)
1995	*Elephant Journeys*	
1995	*Warts and All*	Survival, Barbara Tyack
1995	*Congo*	Paramount Pictures. 2nd Unit Simon Trevor
1996	*The Leopard Son*	Hugo van Lawick. Discovery Productions feature film
1996	*Cheetahs: the winning streak*	Discovery
1996	*The Lions' Pride*	Discovery
1996	*Fifi's Boys*	Partridge Films
1996	*Savage Paradise*	Nature Conservation Films, Hugo van Lawick
1996	*Wildscreen*	BBC Mike Beynon
1996	*Pygmy Chimpanzees, the Last Great Ape*	BBC
1996	*Hippos out of Water*	BBC *Widlife On One* Martha Holmes
1996	*Dawn to Dusk (Serengeti)*	BBC
1996	*Small Cat Country*	BBC
1996	*Gorillas*	Moses Films
1996	*Wild Chimpanzees*	Partridge Films
1996	*Nakuru, an Island in Africa*	ZDF
1996	*Tale of the Tides*	Deeble and Stone
1996	*Lions in Trouble*	Living Planet Productions
1996	*Mzee, a Chimp that's a Problem*	Living Planet Productions
1996	*The Flamingo and the Shoebill*	Living Planet Productions
1996	*Crowned Eagle, King of the Forest*	Living Planet Productions
1996	*Crowned Crane, Queen of the Marsh*	Living Planet Productions
1996	*Wild Guide*	Michael Hoff Productions
1996	*Africa's Elephant Kingdom (Imax)*	Mullion Creek Productions
1996	*The Ultimate Guide to Elephants*	Windfall Films
1996	*Nature*	WNET 12
1996	*Big Cat Diary 1*	BBC
1996	*Outdoor Life*	Peter Henning Productions
1996	*Imax Elephant Promo*	Mullion Creek Productions
1996	*Origins of Man*	Spiegel TV
1996	*Congo*	National Geographic
1996	*Slave to Nature*	BBC Radio

1996	Ecotourism	CTV Toronto
1996	Wildlife	Leonard Rue Enterprises
1996	Wildlife	Titan TV
1996	Crocodile Special	BBC
1996	Baboon Tales	Tamarin Productions
1996	The Ultimate Guide to Big Cats	Scorer Associates
1996	Wild Cats	Partridge Films
1996	Kenya Safari	Interstar TV
1996	Big Cat Diary Titles	Burrell Durant & Hifle
1996	The Really Wild Show	BBC
1996	Great Safaris	Jim Burroughs Associates
1996	From Kilimanjaro to the Coast	American Adventure Productions
1996	From Flowers to Rhinos	Fotoplus Productions
1996	Africa's Forgotten Elephants	Scorer Associates
1996	Haya Safari	Boreales
1996	Antelopes	Zebra Films
1996	Explorer Wraps	National Geographic
1996	Gladys, the African Vet	Cunliffe & Franklin Productions for BBC
1996	The Ultimate Guide to Horses	Taurus Productions for Discovery
1996	Eagle Special	John Downer Productions for BBC
1996	Maneaters of Tsavo, the Real Story	Bioscope Productions
1996	Kenya Safari	WDR
1996	Flamingoes and Elephants	Wolfgang Bayer
1996	The Life of Birds	BBC mega series
1996	Coming of Age with Elephants	Joyce Poole
1996	Musiara Marsh	Londolozi Productions
1996	The Ghost and the Darkness	2nd unit filmed in Kenya by Jack Couffer
1996	Dances with Bees	AEFF Simon Trevor
1997	Tomorrow's World	BBC
1997	Really Wild Show series 12	BBC Megan Lander (Maasai school run, wildebeest migration, snake man, flamingoes Bogoria, chimp boy, ostrich, L Naivasha, elephant orphanage)
1997	Duma the Cheetah	Simon King
1997	Bands on the Run	BBC Wildlife on One

1997	Africa's Paradise of Thorns	National Geographic
1997	The Cheetah Family	Nature Conservation Films/ National Geographic
1997	Serengeti Symphony	Discovery/Nature Conservation Films
1997	Brothers in Arms	Londolozi Productions
1997	Great Safaris	Quest Productions
1997	The Nile (IMAX)	National Geographic
1997	Wild Animals	Titan TV
1997	Wild Guide	Partridge Films
1997	Chimpanzee Diary	BBC
1997	Buffalos	Partridge Films
1997	Spirits in Stone	Quest Productions
1997	The Battle of the Sexes	BBC John Sparks
1997	Animal Minds (chimpanzees)	Green Umbrella
1997	Samburu	Barrett Productions
1997	Serengeti	ZDF
1997	Flying Vets	Tros
1997	Wild Pets of Ol Jogi	Wild Things
1997	Show Me the Honey	Wild Things
1997	Animal Orphanage	3BM TV
1997	Big Cat Diary Update	BBC
1997	Bamburi Nature Trail	Think Tank
1997	Jackals	Paneikon SRL
1997	Host Wraps	Paneikon SRL
1997	Amazing Earth	Fulcrum Productions
1997	Animal Minds	Green Umbrella
1997	Supernatural	John Downer Productions
1997	Elephant Shrews	National Geographic (promo by Linda Bell)
1997	Earth Story	BBC London
1997	The Making of Africa's Elephant Kingdom	Discovery
1997	Animal Weapons	Wild Visuals
1997	Champions of the Wild: elephants	Omni Productions
1997	Champions of the Wild: rhinos	Omni Productions
1997	Jackals	BBC
1997	Animal Zone	BBC
1997	Crocodiles	Green Umbrella

1997	*Hyenas, Heroes or Villains?*	BBC
1997	*The State of the Planet*	BBC
1997	*The Human Body*	BBC London
1997	*Animal Minds: baboons*	Green Umbrella
1997	*Queleas*	Partridge Films
1997	*Being There*	BBC
1997	*River Dinosaur*	Londolozi Productions
1997	*Best of Wildlife Film Makers*	National Geographic
1997	*Wildlife*	Wild Things
1997	*Animal Minds: elephants*	Green Umbrella
1997	*Wildlife*	Flat Dog Productions
1997	*21st Century Safari*	BBC
1997	*Mongooses: wilderness warriors*	
1997	*Hell or High Water*	Survival, Simon Trevor
1998	African Environmental Film Foundation formed	Simon Trevor
1998	*The Meanest Animal in the World*	Survival Simon Trevor
1998	*Champions of the Wild: monkey matriarchs*	Omni Productions, Rudi Kovanic
1988	*Champions of the Wild: elephant matriarchs*	Omni Productions, Rudi Kovanic
1998	*Cheetah in a Hot Spot*	Tigress Productions/BBC
1998	*Uncharted Africa*	Flat Dog Productions SA
1998	*Approaching a Coincidence*	T & C Films
1998	*Really Wild Show*	BBC Martyn Suker (Giraffe manor, Bamburi park)
1998	*Frogs*	Survival Anglia
1998	*A Day in the Life of the Planet*	BBC
1998	*Living with El Nino*	BBC
1998	*Big Cat Diary 2*	BBC
1998	*Supernature*	John Downer Productions Dir. Adrian Warren
1998	*New Sanctuaries*	Tele Images
1998	*Champions of the Wild (rhinos)*	Omni Productions
1998	*To Walk with Lions*	Feature starring Richard Harris
1998	*Elephants*	Wall to Wall
1998	*The Lion Queen*	BBC
1998	*Living Edens: Ngorongoro*	Last Refuge Productions Dir. Adrian Warren
1998	*Rivers of Life* (IMAX)	Graphic Films

1998	*Jane Goodall*	KTCA TV
1998	*Dian Fossey*	Cunliffe & Franklyn Productions
1998	*Africa Quest*	US Classrooms
1998	*Anthropology*	Beyond Productions
1998	*Orphans*	Piper Films
1998	*Crocodiles*	Londolozi Productions
1998	*Mt Kilimanjaro*	Atalante, Paris
1998	*The Pink Caravan*	Titan TV
1998	*Snows of Kilimanjaro (IMAX)*	Pascale Blais Productions
1998	*Triumph of Life*	Green Umbrella
1998	*Big Cat Diary Update*	BBC
1998	*QED: Bongo*	BBC London
1998	*Painted Horses*	Cicada films
1998	*Weaver Birds*	Wildscreen films
1998	*Dung Beetles*	BBC
1998	*The Great Ruaha River (Hell or hot water, drought of the century)*	African Environmental Filmmakers' Foundation, Simon Trevor
1998	*Bug World*	Survival Anglia
1998	*Animal Zone*	BBC
1998	*Lost Africa*	Quest Productions
1998	*Scavengers of the Savannah*	St Thomas Productions
1998	*Animal Zone*	BBC
1998	*Zone Sauvage*	Leo Productions
1998	*Maneaters of Tsavo*	Kurtis Productions
1998	*Why Dogs Smile & Chimpanzees Cry*	Fleisherfilm
1998	*Elephants or Ivory*	BBC Horizon
1998	*Johnny Morris on Safari*	Match Frame
1998	*Lions*	Wall to Wall
1998	*Lions, Spy in the Den*	John Downer Productions
1998	*Champions of the Wild: lions*	Omni Productions
1998	*Project Life Lion*	GW Trust/Disney
1998	*Champions of the Wild: giraffes*	Omni Productions
1998	*Champions of the Wild: baboons*	Omni Productions
1998	*Michael Palin's Hemingway Adventure*	Prominent TV
1998	*Mzima, Haunt of the River Horse*	Deeble and Stone
1998	*Living with Hippos (making of Mzima)*	Deeble and Stone

1998	*The Gates of Hell*	Nature Conservation Films
1998	*Treasures of the Wild, Search for the Big Cats*	
1998	*Ray Mears World of Survival*	BBC
1999	*Das enbe des lowenvaters*	
1999	*The State of the Planet*	BBC
1999	*Triumph of Life*	Green Umbrella
1999	*Warthogs, Hogging the Limelight*	BBC *Wildlife on One*
1999	*Zone Sauvage*	Leo Productions
1999	*The Dawn of Man*	BBC WOO
1999	*African Islands*	Paneikon SRF
1999	*Hyrax, Little Brother of the Elephant*	BBC *Wildlife on One*
1999	*Uncharted Africa*	Flat Dog Productions
1999	*George Adamson*	Top TV
1999	*Blue Peter*	BBC
1999	*Pelicans*	Naturfilm Produktions
1999	*Return to the Wild: giraffes*	Café Productions
1999	*AFRICA*	Tigress Productions
1999	*The Big Squeeze*	Partridge Films
1999	*The Great Croc Trail*	Partridge Films
1999	*Saving Endangered Species*	Ramm Entertainment
1999	*Big Cat Diary Update*	BBC
1999	*Volcanos*	95 West
1999	*Chimpanzees*	Free Spirit Films
1999	*Wild Africa: savannahs*	BBC
1999	*Cats of Lamu*	National Geographic
1999	*Sinbad's Journey*	Becker Entertainment
1999	*Aerials*	The Talking Picture Co
1999	*Wild Africa: mountains*	BBC
1999	*The Arid Heart*	Discovery/NHNZ/NHK
1999	*Brothers in Arms*	Londolozi Productions
1999	*Bush Meat Trade*	Ashley Hayland
1999	*Ostriches*	Green Umbrella
1999	*Flamingoes and Elephants*	Tigress Productions
1999	*Jane Goodall's Wild Chimpanzees* (IMAX)	Science North
1999	*Ivory Wars*	BBC Panorama
1999	*Clever Dicks*	BBC

1999	*Champions of the Wild: a good vet in Africa*	Omni Productions
1999	*Champions of the Wild: lions*	Omni Productions
1999	*Champions of the Wild: giraffes*	Omni Productions
1999	*Champions of the Wild: baboons*	Omni Productions
1999	*Champions of the Wild: eagles*	Omni Productions
1999	*Flip Flotsam*	Oliff & Bateman
1999	*Elephant Kingdom*	AEFF Simon Trevor
1999	*Wisdom of the Wild*	Argo Films
1999	*Into Africa: the Swahili coast*	Wall to Wall
1999	*Military Monkeys*	ZDF
1999	*Wild Africa: coasts*	BBC
1999	*Vets in the Wild*	BBC, Michael Massey
1999	*Supernatural*	John Downer Productions
1999	*Natural Passions: Dr Rhino*	Omni Productions
1999	*Flying Hooves, Fleeting Shadows*	
1999	*The Greatest Wildlife Show on Earth*	Pathfinder Films, Philip Cayford
1999	*An Animal's World: lion*	
1999	*An Animal's World: elephant*	
1999	*Saga*	JLR Productions
2000	*I Dreamed of Africa*	Dir. Hugh Hudson
2000	*Intimate Enemies: lions and buffalo*	Tigress Productions
2000	*Africa: making of*	Tigress Productions
2000	*Chimpanzees*	Epo Films
2000	*Pollution*	Antelope Films
2000	*Elephants*	@ Bristol
2000	*Cousins*	BBC Miles Barton, Charlotte Uhlenbroek
2000	*Vets in Practice*	BBC
2000	*I Dreamed of Africa, Documentary*	Atlantic Productions
2000	*Really Wild Show*	BBC
2000	*Rhinos, Built to Last?*	BBC
2000	*Evolution*	WGBH
2000	*Living Dangerously*	BBC
2000	*Big Cat Diary 3*	BBC
2000	*Global Trek*	Pilot Films
2000	*The People's Planet*	Antelope Films

2000	The Life of Mammals	BBC mega series
2000	Dongo Kundu	Worldwide Film Expedition
2000	The Future of the African Elephant	Epo Films
2000	Living with the Elephants	BBC
2000	Hippos	Moonlighting
2000	Echo of the Elephants, the Final Chapter	Mike Birkhead Productions for BBC
2000	Lions	Zambezi Films
2000	Nakuru	Atomic Productions
2000	Lion Battlefields	BBC
2000	Mt Kenya	Triple Echo
2000	Safari	STE
2000	Return to the Forest	Nature Conservation Films
2000	Deadly African Snakes with Steve Irwin	Partridge Films
2000	Champions of the Wild: hyena	Omni Productions
2000	The People's Planet	
2000	Playing in Savage Paradise	Nature Conservation Films
2000	The Horse with Stripes	Hans Klingel fot Ch 5
2000	Untamed Africa	
2001	Kenya's Hidden Crabs	BBC Marguerite smits van oyen, Gavin Thurston
2001	Threads of Life	
2001	Really Wild Show	(Zebras, Lewa; eles Tsavo; Omni & Digby rhinos at Lewa; hippo Naivasha; kudu Lewa, vervets Diani, honeyguides Lewa, Colobus Diani, baby big cats, Nairobi orphanage, maneaters of Tsavo)
2001	Watamu/Arabuko-Sokoke	BBC Chris Packham
2001	Kilimanjaro (IMAX)	Kilimanjaro Productions
2001	Crocodiles	National Geographic
2001	Koobi Fora	Tangram Films
2001	Swahili	Along Mekong
2001	Mara	Kurtis Productions
2001	Cats of Lamu	National Geographic
2001	Genetic Plants	NOVA
2001	Toyota World of Wildlife	Partridge Films
2001	Leipzig Zoo	Patocka Films
2001	Mara Safari	Readers Digest films

2001	Champions of the Wild: zebra	Omni Productions
2001	Champions of the Wild: hippos	Omni Productions
2001	Millennium Man	JWM
2001	Giraffes	Pangolin Pictures
2001	The Hunt for Virgo	BBC
2001	Origins of Man	BBC Horizon
2001	Dogs	BBC
2001	Elephant Translocation	National Geographic
2001	Jules Silvester	Welland Davidson
2001	Nairobi National Park	NDR
2001	City Slickers	BBC
2001	Nakuru	Paneikon SRL
2001	Turkana	Aland Pictures
2001	Flower Labels	Media 3
2001	Survivor	CBS 60 minutes
2001	The Great Outdoors	Australia Channel 7
2001	Ape Man	Granada Media
2001	Kiwaiyu	Atomic Productions
2001	Travel Promotion	African Odyssey
2001	Crocodiles with Mulji Modha	Flying Scotsman Films
2001	Origins of Man	BBC Horizon
2001	Where We Come From	Uden
2001	Animal Minds	BBC
2001	Gene Machine	BBC Science
2001	Be an Animal	BBC
2001	Extreme Animals	BBC
2001	The Skin We Are In	New Pony
2001	The Crossing	BBC TNW Michael Bright, Hugh Miles
2001	Untamed Africa	
2001	Out in Nature: homosexual behaviour in the animal kingdom	St Thomas Productions, Bertrand Loyer
2001	Buffalo, the African Boss	
2001	Africa Special	Discovery Canada
2001	The Ape that Took Over the World	BBC Horizon
2001	The Jeff Corwin Experience	
2002	Nguva, the Forgotten Mermaid	Quite Bright Films

2002	*Elephants, Spy in the Herd*	John Downer Productions
2002	*Ice World*	Wall to Wall
2002	*Life of Mammals Promo*	BBC
2002	*Elephant Cave*	BBC *The Natural World*, Justine Evans
2002	*Knockenkrieg*	Spiegel TV
2002	*Coastal Kayas*	Norbert Rottcher
2002	*Tarangire*	Nature Conservation Films
2002	*The African King*	Nature Conservation Films
2002	*Toyota World of Wildlife*	BBC
2002	*Daphne Sheldrick*	Concept TV
2002	*The Lioness and the Oryx*	Origination and Design
2002	*The Miracle Lioness*	BBC
2002	*Wanted, Dead or Alive*	AEFF Simon Trevor
2002	*Running Dry*	AEFF Simon Trevor
2002	*Africa*	Paul Dektor
2002	*Arts Project*	Eisinga
2002	*Haydn Turner's Wildlife Challenge: big cats*	Tigress Productions
2002	*Haydn Turner's Wildlife Challenge: flamingos*	Tigress Productions
2002	*Haydn Turner's Wildlife Challenge: wildebeest*	Tigress Productions
2002	*Human Instinct*	BBC Science
2002	*Winning Dads*	BBC
2002	*Children's Programme*	CBBC
2002	*Animal Talk*	BBC
2002	*Lewa Marathon*	Transworld Sport
2002	*Water Hyacinth*	Atomic Productions
2002	*Big Cat Diary 4*	BBC
2002	*Born to Be Wild: giraffes on the move*	BBC, Michael Massey
2002	*A Keeper's Diary*	AEFF Simon Trevor
2002	*The Call of Africa*	New Atlantis Line
2002	*Jeder Wind hat seine Reise*	
2002	*Nile Croc: the ultimate crocodile*	National Geographic
2003	*Maasai*	Presentable Films
2003	*Crocodiles*	BBC
2003	*Kenya Wildlife Service*	Megaherz
2003	*Wild Night In*	BBC
2003	*Awards: Daphne Sheldrick*	BBC

2003	*Culture and Ecology*	ITE/AIT
2003	*Mara Game Count*	Origination and Design
2003	*Daphne Sheldrick*	Beyond Productions
2003	*Turkana*	Force Four
2003	*Jeff Corwin*	Popular Arts
2003	*Fast Track to Freeedom*	BBC
2003	*Maasai Cattle to USA*	BBC News
2003	*Harbours of Africa*	Point du Jour
2003	*Lewa Wildlife Conservancy*	Gratis 7
2003	*Sweetwaters*	Norwegian Broadcasting
2003	*Slowliness*	Degn Film
2003	*Animals*	St Thomas Productions
2003	*Queen of Trees*	Deeble & Stone
2003	*Elephants*	HD Net
2003	*Ming Dynasty in Africa*	Paladin Invision
2003	*Lokkichoggio*	BBC
2003	*Transmara*	WWF
2003	*Africa Journey*	Phoenix TV
2003	*Big Cat Diary 5*	BBC
2003	*Animal Annie*	Kajak TV
2003	*Lions*	National Geographic
2003	*Journey of Life*	BBC
2003	*Lions of Nairobi National Park*	Atomic Productions
2003	*Massive Nature: wildebeest*	BBC
2003	*Trek*	John Downer Productions
2003	*The Way We Went Wild*	BBC Scotland
2003	*Turkana*	SWR
2003	*Dragons Alive*	BBC
2003	*Time Machine*	BBC
2003	*Mau Forest, FOMAWA*	Andrew Nightingale
2003	*Green Belt Movement*	Back 2 Back
2003	*Sleeping with the Elephant*	Canadian Broadcasting Corporation
2003	*Alistair McGowan Goes Wild with Rhinos*	BBC
2003	*Journey to Planet Earth: hot zones*	Screenscope Inc
2003	*Journey to Planet Earth: seas of grass*	Screenscope Inc
2003	4 May	Michaela Denis died

2004	*Pride*	John Downer Productions (animated)
2004	*Lion, out of Africa?*	BBC *The Natural World*, Ingrid Kvale
2004	*The Journey of Life*	BBC
2004	*Really Wild Show*	BBC Nigel Pope
2004	*Elephant Diaries 1*	BBC
2004	*Massive Nature: flamingoes*	BBC
2004	*Elephants of Kilimajaro*	Nature Conservation Films/National Geographic
2004	*Lions*	Beyond Productions
2004	*Daphne Sheldrick*	Care for the wild
2004	*Be the Creature: cheetah*	Kratts Productions
2004	*Turkana*	National Geographic
2004	*Michaela's Wildlife Challenge*	Two Hands
2004	*Elephants*	BBC Radio
2004	*Elephant Diaries Update*	BBC
2004	*Ray Mears' Survival*	BBC
2004	*Chelsea Flower Show*	BBC
2004	*Clean fuel* (UN)	Origination and Design
2004	*Samburu Elephants*	BBC
2004	*Lions, the Last Roar*	Australia 60 minutes
2004	*Bella the Leopard*	BBC
2004	*Wildlife*	Wild Doc
2004	*Lions*	Doc TV
2004	*Really Wild Show*	BBC
2004	*Baboons*	Stanford University
2004	*Bacilos in Kenya*	Explora Films
2004	*Aerials*	Unearth Africa
2004	*Big Cat Week*	BBC
2004	*Turkana Art*	Vignette Films
2004	*Driver Ants*	BBC
2004	*African Assassin*	BBC
2004	*Earthwatch*	Bahati Productions
2004	*Bloopers*	St Thomas Productions
2004	*Elephants*	Intrepid Films
2004	*Chimpanzee Sanctuary*	Swedish TV
2004	*The Nature of Shopping: the real price of a rose*	Living Planet Productions

2004	Elephant, Return to the Wild	NCF/Animal Planet
2004	The Monkey Hunters	NCF/National Geographic
2004	Really Wild Show	BBC
2004	The Revengeful Elephant (aka Predator CSI: revenge of the elephants)	Tigress Productions for National Geographic
2004	Fascination Earth	ZDF
2004	Black Rhino, on the Brink	AEFF Simon Trevor
2004	Maasai, Warriors of the Rain (guerriers de la pluie)	Pascale Plisson
2004	Terzeit: lions	
2004	Flying Zebra	Frankfurt Zoological Society/ZDF
2005	DNA	National Geographic
2005	Jeff Corwin	Tigress Productions
2005	Nick News	Lucky Duck Productions/Nikolodeon
2005	Toki's Tale	BBC
2005	Ants	BBC
2005	The Planet	Charon Film AB
2005	Life in the Undergrowth	BBC mega series
2005	Animal Park	Endemol
2005	Mara: Africa's river of destiny	Peter Glaub Productions
2005	Nairobi National Park	Wild Doc
2005	Naked Mole Rats	Gruppe 5
2005	Daphne Sheldrick	Care for the Wild
2005	Philadelphia Zoo	WPTI TV
2005	Rosie and the Mole Rats	Taglicht Media
2005	Cheza and Sala	BBC
2005	Photographers at Work (J Scott)	Coast House Productions
2005	Lamu	Time Frame
2005	Last Chance to Save the Rhino	Tiger Aspect
2005	An Eye for an Elephant	Mike Birkhead Productions
2005	Saba DH	Animal Planet
2005	Animal Park	Endemol
2005	White Lion	David Adams
2005	Big Cat Week	BBC
2005	UNEP	Bach Film
2005	Promo	Tusk Trust
2005	Footprints on the Water	NCF/Animal Planet

2005	*Worlds Apart*	Rubicon
2005	*Serengeti Shall Not Die*	Gest Productions Tanzania
2005	*A Zoo Keeper's Diary*	AEFF Simon Trevor
2005	*Planet Earth: aerials*	BBC
2005	*Africa Within*	Saira Essa
2005	*Planet Earth: cheetahs*	BBC
2005	*Africa Within*	East Mosaic
2005	*Quench the Thirst*	Frog Pond Productions
2005	*Wildlife*	Channel 1 network
2005	*Elephant Diaries: Christmas special*	BBC NHU
2005	*Heart of a Lioness*	Animal Planet
2006	Joan Root murdered at her home in Naivasha, Kenya	
2006	*The Orphanage*	CBS 60 minutes
2006	*The Ape Trade*	Environmental News Trust
2006	*Big Cat Uncut*	BBC
2006	*Walk With Me*	Maasai Power & Education Project
2006	*Survival*	Darlow Smithson
2006	*Search for the Perfect Picture*	Kenya Tourist Board
2006	*Daphne Sheldrick*	Care for the Wild
2006	*Fishing*	WWF Sweden
2006	*Elephant Diaries 2*	BBC
2006	*The Planet*	Charon Film AB
2006	*Animal Park*	Endemol
2006	*KWS Projects*	Etienne Oliff
2006	*The Indianapolis Prize*	Pathway Productions
2006	*Wild Vets*	Tigress Productions
2006	*Roses*	Spiegel TV
2006	*A Place in the Wild*	Endemol
2006	*Saving Planet Earth*	BBC
2006	*Born to Be Wild*	Endemol
2006	*From Cairo to Cape Town*	ARD/WDR
2006	*Big Cat Week*	BBC
2006	*Mission Africa*	Diverse Bristol
2006	*Maneaters*	Pangolin Pictures
2006	*Flamingos*	Steel Spyda
2006	*Smithsonian Project*	Sonnett Media

2006	*Wildebeest Migration*	Australia 60 minutes
2006	*Camp Kenya*	Strix TV
2006	*Weather Report*	Sienna Films
2006	*Return of the Plagues*	Taglicht Media
2006	*Elephants*	Passion Pictures
2006	*Extreme Sculpture*	Creative Touch Films
2006	*Survival*	Diverse Bristol
2006	*Lions*	Passion Pictures
2006	*Finding James Leopard*	Southern Star
2006	*The Best of Saba*	BBC
2006	*Saba and the Rhino's Secret*	Passion Wild
2006	*Travel to the Edge with Art Wolfe*	Edge of the earth productions
2006	*Enjoye Special*	France 2
2006	*Natural Security*	AEFF Simon Trevor
2006	*Rain in a Dry Land*	Dir. Anne Makepeace
2006	*Demain La Terre*	France2 + SEP, Yann Arthus Bertrand
2006	*Les animaux amoureux*	MC4 Productions, Paris (35mm) Dir. Laurent Charbonnier
2007	*3 Peaks, 3 Weeks*	Serac Adventure Films
2007	*Game Over: conservation in Kenya*	Canadian Broadcasting
2007	*Crowned Eagles*	David Gulden
2007	*Women of the Tribe*	Diverse Bristol
2007	*Elephants*	Care for the Wild
2007	*Elephants*	The Gamma Project
2007	*Life: cheetahs*	BBC
2007	*Are We There Yet?*	Sinking Ship Productions
2007	*Big Cat: lions*	BBC
2007	*Crimson Wing*	Natural Light Films for Disney Nature
2007	*Pastoralists*	University of Bergen
2007	*The Long Way Down*	Big Earth & Elixir Films
2007	*Elephant Shrew, Spirit of the Forest*	Taglicht Media
2007	*Living with Elephants 1*	BBC
2007	*Saving Planet Earth: running wild*	BBC
2007	*Stress, Portrait of a Killer*	National Geographic
2007	*Jeff Corwin: lions*	Pioneer TV
2007	*Mara Water*	No Opportunity Wasted

2007	Bongos	David Gulden
2007	Naabi – A Hyena Princess	BBC TNW, Charlie Hamilton James
2007	Life: elephant shrews	BBC
2007	Conservation at Kiwaiyu	Emanuel
2007	Africa Within	Saira Essa
2007	Insects	Interaktive Kommunication
2007	Maasai Beads	Left Right TV
2007	Ecotourism	Elephant & Cie
2007	Fake Medicines	Canadian Broadcasting
2007	Wild Dog Island	NCF/Animal Planet
2007	African Bambi	NCF/Animal Planet
2007	Holiday Show	GMTV
2007	Climate Change	EC1 Productions
2007	Kenya Holiday	Familie
2007	The Genius of Charles Darwin	WCI Productions
2007	Auf und Davon	WW Productions
2007	Living with Elephants 2	BBC
2007	Africa's Greatest Explorer	Unicorn Productions, Mike Hacker
2007	My Life with Animals (Saba DH)	
2008	Boomerang	Elzivir Films, Yann Arthus Bertrand
2008	Trouble in Paradise	Raw TV
2008	Alternative Medicines	Rockhopper TV
2008	Life: flamingos	BBC
2008	Living with Elephants 3	BBC
2008	The Evolution of Nakedness	BBC Horizon
2008	Migrations: white eared cob	National Geographic
2008	Migrations: wildebeest	National Geographic
2008	Human/Elephant Conflict	Darlow Smithson/Discovery
2008	Human Origins & Climate Change	Shining Red Productions
2008	Big Cat Live	BBC
2008	Big Cat Live Promo/Cbeebies	BBC
2008	Big Cat Feature	Big Cat Ltd/Disney Nature
2008	Big Cat Titles	Burrell Durant and Hifle
2008	Cbeebies	BBC Children's
2008	Cheetahs, Against All Odds	NCF/France 5
2008	The Fawn Identity	NCF/France 5

Africa's Big Five and other Wildlife Filmmakers ◆ 157

2008	*Canon: insects*	Coast House Productions
2008	*Daphne Sheldrick's Orphans*	MDR
2008	*The Great Rift*	BBC
2008	*The Great Rift*	ORF
2008	*Voyage of Time*	Sycamore Films, dir. Terrence Malick
2008	*Mara Ecosystem*	Intervista
2008	*Last Chance to See*	BBC Cardiff
2008	*Daphne Sheldrick's Orphans*	GMTV
2008	*Big Cat Live Highlights*	BBC
2008	*Murder on the Lake*	Firefly Films
2008	*Changing Lives*	Shadow Industries
2008	*Turkana Nomads*	True Nature Films
2008	*Kilimanjaro, Despite All Odds*	Polish TV
2008	*Grooten Terug*	Eyeworks BV
2008	*Solio Translocation*	Green Footprint, Tz
2008	*60 Minutes: lions*	CBS 60 minutes
2008	*Earth Flight*	John Downer Productions
2008	*Architects of Change*	Lato Sensu Productions
2008	*Lions*	Exploraction
2008	*Echo and the Elephants of Amboseli*	Mike Birkhead Productions for Animal Planet
2009	*Evolution*	Atlantic Productions
2009	*Afraid of the Dark*	Wholly Cow Productions
2009	*Migrations*	National Geographic
2009	*The Secret Leopards*	BBC
2009	*Inspiration*	AEFF
2009	*Echo, an unforgettable elephant*	Mike Birkhead Productions
2009	*Primates*	Great primate handshake
2009	*Mara*	CBS 60 minutes
2009	*Lewa*	The Nature Conservancy
2009	*Daphne Sheldrick's Orphans*	Polish TVN
2009	*Baboons*	Ammonite
2009	*Wildebeest Migration*	Aquavision
2009	*100 Heartbeats*	NBC
2009	*Africa*	BBC
2009	*No Water, no life*	Alison Jones

2009	Mara	Intervista, Reinhard Radke
2009	Human Planet (Samburu)	BBC
2009	The Wonders of Planet Earth	Cicada Films
2009	Lions	Ammonite
2009	Geologic Journey	Canadian Broadcasting
2009	Born Free Revisited	Icon Films
2009	Climate Change	True Nature Films
2009	3D Test Shoot	Deeble & Stone
2009	Northern White Rhinos	BBC Last chance to see

Index

A

Adamson, George   48, 58, 60, 136, 138, 141, 147
Adamson, Joy and George   58
Adamson, Joy   60, 126, 127, 129, 130, 134, 141
African Environmental Filmmakers' Foundation   82, 145, 146
Aitchison, John   74
Akeley, Carl   2, 18, 31, 32, 33, 35, 41, 42, 119-121
Akeley, Delia   19
American Museum of Natural History   18, 22, 32, 36, 42, 119-121
Attenborough, David   4, 54, 59, 68, 80, 83, 99, 104, 111, 127
Austin, Harold   28, 30

B

Barnes, Jim   40
Bartlett, Des and Jen   73
Bartlett, Des   6, 54, 64, 69, 76, 83, 97, 98, 125-128
Binks, HK ("Pop")   2, 18, 21, 22, 23, 119, 120
Booth, Edwina   40, 47, 122
Born Free   58, 59, 60, 99, 127, 129, 131, 159
Boswall, Jeffrey   24, 107, 112, 133
Boyce, William   2, 18, 19, 20, 85, 119
Breakston, George   62, 124, 126, 127
Brock, Richard   74, 80, 100, 101, 102, 131, 132, 134, 138
Buck, Frank   51
Buxton, Aubrey   72, 73, 100
Buxton, Cindy   73, 100, 131, 133, 134, 139

C

Campbell , Bob   68, 69, 85, 98, 102, 129-136, 138
Carey, Harry   40, 46, 122
Carr Hartley, Thomas   47, 60, 62, 99
Christian   48, 59, 60, 80, 112, 131
Colbeck, Martyn   106
Cottar, Bud   26, 32, 39
Cottar, Charles   2, 25, 26, 27, 39